Letters
from the
HOLY GROUND

❧

Seeing God
Where You Are

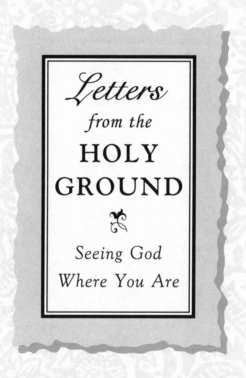

Letters
from the
HOLY GROUND

Seeing God
Where You Are

LORETTA ROSS-GOTTA

SHEED & WARD
Franklin, Wisconsin

The mission of Sheed & Ward, an apostolate of the Priests of the Sacred Heart, a Catholic religious congregation, is to publish books of contemporary impact and enduring merit in Catholic Christian thought and action. The books published, however, reflect the opinions of their authors and are not meant to represent the official position of the Priests of the Sacred Heart.

2000

Sheed & Ward
7373 South Lovers Lane Road
Franklin, Wisconsin 53132
1-800-266-5564

Cover and interior design by Robin Booth
Author photo by Wichers Photography, Topeka, Kansas

Library of Congress Cataloging-in-Publication Data
Ross-Gotta, Loretta.
    Letters from the holy ground : seeing God where you are / Loretta Ross-Gotta.
    p. cm.
    ISBN 1-58051-084-1 (alk. paper)
1. Spiritual life–Christianity. 2. Ross-Gotta, Loretta. I. Title.
BV4501.2 .R675 2000
248.4'851–dc21   00-056334

Americans seek the quick fix for spiritual as well as physical pain.
That conversion is a life long process is the least they want to hear.

—KATHLEEN NORRIS, *Dakota*

A contemplative is not someone who takes his prayer seriously,
but someone who takes God seriously, who is famished for the truth,
who seeks to live in generous simplicity in the Spirit.
Perhaps one of the functions of a contemplative is to help other people
by word or merely by example, to become aware
of how much they already love God without knowing it.

—THOMAS MERTON, *The Sign of Jonas*

Dedication

To my mother and father
and the Sacred Heart of Jesus

CONTENTS

• • •

PART VI: Becoming Ordinary 129

PART VII: We Have Eternity 169

ACKNOWLEDGMENTS

• • •

*M*any of these essays have been published in somewhat different form in *Making Haqqodesh*, a publication of the Sanctuary Center for Prayer in Topeka, Kansas. Part of chapter 36 was first published in the readers' chancel drama, *Quem Quaeritis?*, published by the Sanctuary. The prayer at the beginning of chapter 8 was published in *More Than Meets the Eye* by Thomas Greisen, Mary Jo Pedersen, and Ronald Wasikowski, St. Mary's Press, Winona, Minnesota. A small part of chapter 9 was published in *Weavings*, Vol. VIII, No. 9, as "Praying with Christ."

I want to extend special thanks to Marianne and Al Neisser, who generously saw that I would have a place to write, and heartfelt gratitude to Eva and Winston Wheeler, Jerry, Barb, Mike, and John who provided holy ground. I owe a great deal to my friends, donors, directees, and subscribers to the Sanctuary newsletter, *Making Haqqodesh*. I am grateful to the Presbytery of Northern Kansas for supporting me in pursuing a nontraditional ministry. Special thanks also to Dixon Junkin and other denomination leaders who offered encouragement early on. I am grateful to Louisville Presbyterian Theological Seminary and their faculty, who provided me with an excellent theological education and the freedom to explore my creativity in 1978–1981. Thanks also to the faculty of the Shalem Institute. I am grateful to the parishes I served, which welcomed and nourished me and taught me about their love for God. Special thanks to Crestview United Methodist Church. I want to thank the founding board members of the Sanctuary who gave so freely of their energy, imagination, and love. Thanks also to Joan, Susan, Faith, Joyce, Leslie, Helen, Boyd, Margaret, and Evelyn, who hung in with me through thick and thin. Thank you to my writers' group, Judy, Victor, and Mitch. Blessings to Sister Margaret Dorgan and her gentle Carmelite encouragement. Thank you to Jeff Nichols. Thank you to Marguerite Thompson and Jeremy Langford for their support and vision. Thank you to Edward W. Schmidt, S.J., for his sensitive, careful editing and to Kass Dotterweich for her guiding hand. Thank you to my wonderful extended family—and to the loves of my life, Peter, and our daughters, Diana and Cicelia, who more than once said, "Mom, I think you need to go to the hermitage and pray."

PROLOGUE

• • •

*I*n the beginning I woke in the night gripped with fear. I felt as I did when I was first pregnant. I had gone and done something that was going to change my life forever. It was so frightening and impossible that I hoped people would talk me out of it.

I wasn't nearly this frightened when I enrolled in seminary at age thirty-three. I had already earned a master's degree in theater, had taught for ten years in various schools in the Midwest, and had written and directed theater. And I had fallen in love with God. As I prepared for seminary graduation and ordination, I assumed that my ministry would take the usual shape of parish pastor. But one spring day I confided to a fellow student, "I think I could live by myself in a hut somewhere and pray all the time. But I probably won't get to, because I want it too much. Besides, I'm married. I want to have children. And I'm a Presbyterian."

Shocked, my friend said, "My goodness, I think if anyone would want to do something like that that bad, God would want them to as well."

It would be several years before I dared to believe my friend. I was a wife and pastor, and the life of even a part-time hermit seemed impossible to me. After we graduated my husband and I headed to calls in Kansas, where, pregnant with our first daughter, I was hired as the interim pastor of Seaman

United Church of Christ Church in Topeka. I followed that with other part-time parish ministry.

In 1987, when our second daughter was about three, I sought a permanent job, but every door slammed shut in my face. I had really wanted one particular opening. I lobbied and prayed, stewed and fretted. An older clergyman bluntly advised, "As a woman, you don't have a snowball's chance in hell of getting that job. Besides, it would be wrong for you. It would kill your creativity."

When the rejection finally came, I felt an odd mixture of grief and freedom. Digging down to my deepest truth I told my husband, "Well, you know what I'd really like to do? I'd like to start a ministry of prayer."

"Let's do it," he said. And so we began. For the next three months I woke at night terrified. Nothing I had set out to do before had inspired such a disconcerting mixture of pure gladness and stark fear.

The name of the ministry, the Sanctuary, came to me one day while I was out running. It seemed right. Many churches, I felt, were not true sanctuaries, places of holiness and safety. Sometimes they were places of conflict and pain, shame and blame. Some were rigid, humorless, boring, suspicious of creativity, fearful of intimacy. I came home from my run, pulled out my Hebrew dictionary, and looked up sanctuary. The word is *qodesh*, and it literally means "holy ground."

If necessity is the mother of invention, frustration can be the mother of personal truth and creativity. When my lesser desire was frustrated, disappointment and grief roused me to name and respond to the insistent call to a life of prayer. Following a summons I only partially understood, I turned from the security of professional ministry to pray in a sacrificial and sustained manner.

With the blessing of my presbytery, I began a ministry of spiritual formation to establish, maintain, and nourish holy ground as the place of encounter between God and persons by providing space for prayer and solitude and opportunities for spiritual growth. The ecumenical breadth of the ministry reflected my own Presbyterian, Roman Catholic, Quaker, Amish, and Jewish influences and ancestry.

In October 1998, I announced at a meeting of the Sanctuary board of directors that I was praying one day a week on some wooded land that had been given to us. After I told them that I had arranged to use a room in a local church in bad weather, the board decided to build a cabin on the land. Our goal was to complete it before the snow flew.

On a sunny fall morning, I took the architect's plans out to Wheeler Hardware in tiny Larkinburg, Kansas, to get an estimate. "How much will it cost to build this?" I asked Jerry Wheeler. He took a look at the drawing, rolled it back up, and tossed it on his desk. "Say, Mom and Dad and my brothers and I had a family conference this morning, and we wonder if you would consider another option." I was stunned. What could he mean? I knew Jerry only slightly through his wife, a friend, and I was unaware that he knew anything about what I was up to.

"Come on, get in the car. I want to show you something," Jerry grinned. We drove down the highway a bit, turned south onto a dirt road and then down a winding lane to a lake. "It isn't much. Needs some work. But if you can use it for what you are doing, you can have it."

Standing waist deep in grass, shaking my head in wonder, I saw a stone-and-wood cabin nestled into the side of a hill. Built thirty years before as a family getaway, the place had hosted church picnics, family gatherings, youth groups, fishermen, and quite a few mice. Thus began my relationship with the Wheeler family, givers of holy ground.

From the beginning, the heart of the ministry has been my prayer, which usually has taken place in the one-room hermitage a few miles east of

Holton, Kansas. For over twelve years I have devoted one or two days each week to solitary prayer, with occasional longer periods of up to forty days.

As I explored many different methods and techniques of prayer, prayer became for me a relationship rather than something I do. As with any relationship, there are good days and bad days. Some days I have come to prayer like a lover eagerly rushing to the beloved's arms. Sometimes I have been full of dread and doubt. I have been summoned by an irresistible call that pulled me to my knees like a magnet. I have been so ill or weary that all I could do was show up. Most of the time I come to prayer having deliberately turned toward God and turned away from other demands. Prayer has often involved a gritty choice to not do something else that may seem at the time quite important.

I can't say I feel a whole lot more knowledgeable about prayer or God after all those days and nights. Nor am I able to point with certainty to direct and concrete results. So why do it? Because I have been created for this simple service and there I find joy. I do it for Christ who seems to be pleased to have someone come and spend time with him. I do it for Christ's scattered church. And I do it for those who do not have the time or inclination to pray.

As I began the Sanctuary, I soon felt the need to let others know how things were going. So I started a newsletter as a way to share my experience and to be accountable to those who supported me. This book is a collection of these letters of spiritual guidance. The letters trace my deepening understanding of holy ground and are the fruit of abiding prayer. They often address questions raised by those who came to me for spiritual counsel. The letters explore some of what might be required of a believer in our time. They tell of my struggle to be faithful to the summons to pray and to be responsive to those who looked to me for guidance and to the world at large. Here is what I saw from my hermitage window as the seasons passed, what worried, tormented, and delighted me. You will find talking dogs and rabbits, ducks and children at various ages. You will find a friend's simple witness, the story of a slow twisting journey home to holiness. Maybe you will find something familiar, something you have been looking for. Or better yet, maybe you will look beyond the words to greet the mystery to which they seek to point and glorify.

Take your time reading this book. Each letter offers some aspect of the nature of God and our journey. Choose one that catches your eye. Find a nice quiet spot where you can be yourself. Listen for the sound of the salt sea that is your soul lapping up against the shore of God. Relax and make yourself at home.

What happens to someone who makes a serious commitment to prayer? What is it like to devote substantial portions of time to solitary prayer on a regular basis? I met evil, fought demons, and faced into my own sin. I felt ecstasy and bliss, despair and pain. I became ill for a long time, and then slowly grew well. I whined and complained. I made friends and enemies and mistakes. I dwelt with gratitude and joy. I saw God and live to tell the tale.

Through hot dry summers while the quail called across the pasture, during storms when the wind whipped the lake and shook the cabin, in springs heady sweet with the scent of wild roses, I have been praying for you. May these letters take you a little further onto your own holy ground and into ever deepening intimacy with the Holy One, who loves you more than you can imagine.

PART I

. . .

Holiness Takes Time

The hostess of the retreat center shoved me across the room to an elderly Anglican priest and his wife. "This woman wants to pray all the time; she needs to talk to you," she told them. I haltingly spoke of my desire to pray. The couple, who had founded communities of prayer in India and Hong Kong, gave me some wise advice, and what they said has stayed with me for years. One thing they said was this: *You can't hurry holiness. Holiness takes time.*

At first I was in a big hurry. Some of the time I thought I had already arrived, when I had barely taken the first step. Exhausted and in pain a few years later, I spent an extended period in solitude. During those weeks I saw only my immediate family. I was quite ill for a long time. I lay on the cot on the porch at the hermitage weak and sick. I felt myself dissolve over and over into tiny particles. I dreamed of dead birds. In my dream I met my brother and his family and I told them, "I am going home by way of Turtle Street." I began to think of Turtle Street as the name for this slow journey into the heart of God. My teachers became the dozens of turtles sunning on the shore of the hermitage lake.

Day after day I lay on the cot and dissolved. The wind came up over the pond. The sky closed over me like a steel-gray vault. The wind blew and blew, blowing me like dust into the cracks of the porch, out the door and up the hill across the pasture. The wind lifted and carried me over the ponds, the fields, and the cities. I am going home, I said, by way of Turtle Street.

1989–1990

CHAPTER 1

Seeing God
A Hunger for Holiness

*E*piphany, the twelfth day of Christmas, falls on January 6, at the beginning of the new year. Epiphany is that euphonious span in midwinter, the season of showings, that promises to the swift and clear-eyed no less than a glimpse of divinity, high-tailing it around the corners of our lives. Now that the trees and earth are bare, the God we hunger for will dance naked for those bold enough to believe in such things as incarnation. God will dance naked, will dance wild, will dance free over the frozen land, while we shiver in our veils longing to see with faces bare of illusion, bare of guile. We ache to see with hearts stripped and clean as the maple, whose slim limbs slice space in great, chaste swaths, ordering emptiness, chalking off a place on the floor of heaven for God to trip the light fantastic and leave us all blinded by a graceful shimmy, rubbing our eyes, amazed.

I have set out to pray. I call this endeavor the Sanctuary from the account in Exodus of Moses' encounter with God at the burning bush on holy ground. The Hebrew for *sanctuary* means a sacred place, a holy abode.

I smile to think of us mortals taking it upon ourselves to make sanctuary in the same way we might make a pie or an atom bomb. I figure it keeps God chuckling. For in the end, we can't make much more on our own than a mess. What we do have going for us is our desire. Holy space is created as we seek the Holy One. Our hunger for God hollows out the spaces in our lives and the earth for a sacred meeting with the One who made us. Our willingness to go down into the emptiness, the out-of-the-way spots on the far side of the wilderness thrusts us and our need before burning bushes, where we behold our God and receive our mission.

A friend defines holy ground as "that burning reality which can only be apprehended—which breaks into, really, the present moment (mine or another's)—and which, surprisingly, disorders, reorders, rearranges, resynthesizes all my previous arrangement of reality." Holy ground is not the object, but rather, we are the objects, subject to the flaming Presence who is creating us in the divine image.

I wonder if we seek to create holy space because we cannot not do it. For this we have been created: to carve out impatiently or patiently, skillfully or crudely, a space apart where we meet the One who longs to make our acquaintance. Most of the time we discover holy space in our poverty, our extremity. And it is there in the solitary encounter with Christ—where we ask, "What do you want of me?" and "Who shall I say sends me?"—that commitment and community are born.

What is a devout and holy life? How does one live a contemplative lifestyle with small children? What does it mean to be a Christian at the beginning of a new century? These are some of the questions I take into my prayer.

The late afternoon sun glints on the gnarled branches of the pear tree outside my study window at home. My young daughters, Diana and Cicelia, chase each other up and down the stairs hollering that the other has taken her Barbie doll. I sift through the clutter on my desk and think of you who are reading this.

Each of you is different, unique, like a glittering array of gemstones receiving and reflecting multifaceted light. I am grateful for you and your special form of service, your distinctive response to love, your showing—your epiphany. If we cannot make sanctuary here, now, we cannot make it anywhere. So wherever you are—reading through the mail, sipping your coffee, sighing over the work piled on your desk, sitting in the rocker, wondering what to fix for supper—*reach for it*. A meeting with the One who makes us and all holy places is right before you.

The pear tree is a rat's nest of knotted branches framing the blue sky in small irregular fragments like pieces of stained glass. Step back. Now what do we see here? Is this a tree holding God or is this God holding a tree? The earth is in flames. The seer and the seen keep exchanging costumes. Watch out. We are all platforms for the dancing God. You could become a theater at a moment's notice. Holiness is waiting in your wings. Remember your cue. Open the curtains. Look, quick now, turn upside down, inside out. There it goes tumbling down the stairs, rolling in a fit of giggles across the lawn. God is loose in your world. Reported sightings in Bethlehem and your backyard. Let me know what you catch. I'll keep you posted on my progress.

CHAPTER 2

Prayer Boots
Remembering

I went to Holton Farm and Home Store last week and bought some praying gear—boots, warm socks, and gloves. I chose sturdy waterproof boots from the row of five-buckle galoshes next to the watering troughs. I think I am ready now.

I payed for the boots with money that friends at the church I served gave me when I left. I kept the money, which came attached to the leaves of a prayer plant, for a whole year, not knowing just how to spend it. I considered books, office supplies, and liturgical accouterments. Now I see that proper prayer vestments include boots for walking over this land we call holy.

There is a temptation in the spiritual life to talk about praying, to read about it, to write about it, to attend workshops on it, to preach sermons about it, to feel guilty about not doing it, to build edifices where it is supposed to happen—anything but the scandalously simple yet arduous task of doing it. The one thing the disciples asked Jesus for was not theology or religious education but to teach them how to pray. And Jesus taught them by simply praying. "Here, do it like this," he said.

So I am praying, turning my attention to God more intentionally and for longer periods of time with no particular result in mind beyond a simple open presence to the Holy One. A good deal of this praying is happening on the land. And when you stalk holiness in autumn in Kansas, you need a good pair of boots.

Crouched under a cedar in the rain, sloshing along the winding creek, following the deer trail up the gully, I try to forget myself in prayer that I might remember who I really am. I imagine hiking toward a place of being so self-forgotten in God that I would need nothing external to validate myself. Is it possible to follow the path to holy ground where the communion of prayer alone feeds and sustains the earth and all that dwell thereon?

The more we pray, the more we discover prayer's richness and power, and the more we hunger for it. In its essence prayer is simply paying attention to God. And that turning of the will to God, that choice to attend to God, is how we participate in making holy ground.

Perhaps our task is not so much to make holy space in our lives as to become holy space ourselves. One way of becoming holy ground is to remember who we are. And we are often quite convinced that we most certainly have been forgotten. That may be because we just can't bear the wonder and joy of love. Is that why Love stood before us that night before we killed Love and told us: "This bread is my body . . . this wine, a new promise sealed in my blood. Don't forget!"?

"Don't forget," Love said. "I beg you not to forget. For when you forget, you hang me back on the cross with your lies and self-deception and fear and heedless stampede over my tender presence in all creation."

Still, we do forget. Psychiatrist Gerald May writes that we often do not remember experiences of communion with God because they are so threatening to our egos. The loss of self-definition characteristic of unitive experiences arouses unconscious fear.[1] Wiping off the chalkboard of our spiritual experience, our officious ego scolds, "Let's just forget this ever happened and go back to worshiping me as almighty in your life."

LAST SUMMER A FRIEND and I had a yard sale. For a week I hauled boxes from attic and basement. The children and I lugged baby clothes and infant swings to the dining room, where the kids promptly set up house, sat at a little red table with their knees up to their chins, and had a tea party with the chipped china.

"Remember this? Oh, Mom, look! I remember this cute little dress. I really looked so sweet in it, didn't I?" They chirped away sounding like they were eighty years old.

Each box held wonder. "Look Mom, these beautiful curtains. Can I have them in my room?" Diana crowed, pulling out the tattered remains of the drapes that hung in our first apartment. Cicelia spent two hours playing with the Johnson and Johnson baby blocks.

Later that evening Diana came to me, holding a tiny blue sock to her lip and tucking her head under my arm. Eyes glowing with the rapt smile of one who has seen a vision of angels, she said softly, "Oh, Mommie, I remember me."

Something forgotten, something precious, tender, and pure that Diana called *me* had been recovered for her in that tiny sock. When I asked what she meant, she said, "Well, I just remember myself when I was a baby."

That tiny sock that I could never keep on her foot took her back to a pre-verbal time where she was held, rocked, nursed, sung to. It was a place where *me* dwelled, the essence of her being in the holy ground of the womb. And she stilled her nonstop, seven-year-old inquisitive mind to forget herself, to pay attention and remember who she is: a child cradled in the loving bliss of One who is larger, kinder, and more beautiful than she, and in whom she lives and moves and has her being.

She still crawls in bed with me in the mornings, her coltish long legs and arms poking, thrashing around, giggling, telling me jokes, and saying that she loves me so much. She seeks herself in that safe place, before she bolts into her day of dolls and math and spelling and exuberant surprises. I wish we could all come to our prayer with her trust, playfulness, and devotion.

I stared in shock whenever I passed the dining room with all those cartons brimming over with my past. This is the room where we gather to pray, to recount our salvation history, to remember and receive the Eucharist. Boxes lined the walls. Infant seats and infant carriers and infant bottles and infant sleepers, undershirts and socks spilled all over the space where we sing songs of love to Mary's baby.

My daughters poked about in their past in the room where we come to poke in our past, holding it to the light, turning it over in our palms, wondering what sort of price it would bring, praying God to be merciful.

The sale was one day only. My friend and I sweated it out, swilling ice tea, tallying our profits and losses. During lulls in business, stricken with visions of having to haul all the stuff to the dump, we rushed about with markers, slashing prices. "Everything must go," we resolved, as we paused to fold one last time the sleeper we had laundered and folded so many times we had lost count. We smoothed tiny collars and wrote $.10 on the stickers.

The Age of Aquarius macrame sold, along with the tires, decrepit lounger, ice crusher, and malt maker —but we carted off my friend's wedding gown, the fondue pot, and five or six boxes of baby clothes to the thrift shop.

Afterwards, I picked up hangers and empty boxes from the floor of the room where we, breaking the bread and lifting the cup, do as he asked. Gathering up scraps of newspaper and tags, I saw a little nightie on the table. It was then, forgetting myself in the mystery that rocks us all, and holding to my cheek the soft worn flannel, sweet with baby scent, that *I remembered me*.

ONE OF THE DEEPEST MYSTERIES of holy ground is the mystery of identity. When God meets Moses at the burning bush, the two exchange their identities.

God calls, "Moses, Moses." The call is unique, distinct. There can be no mistaking who is being summoned.

Moses' response is the classic prophetic response to a call from God: "Here I Am." After Moses receives his mission, he presses this burning reality for its identity. "Who shall I say sent me?" he asks.

And God responds, "Tell them that I Am."

Holy ground is the place of exchange where I Am meets Here I Am, where What I Have Been will be transformed by Who I Am Becoming, where I forget what I thought I was and remember I am.

On just about every communion table I have ever seen are carved the words: "Do this in remembrance." The little sacraments of our lives are those graced moments of Holy Communion when we do something prayerfully and in remembrance. We release our grasping and coping. Then bread is transformed into the body of Christ, a blue sock into an angel's wing, and a mortal being into a being in God.

God instructed Moses on Mt. Sinai to make holy garments for Aaron and his sons, including a plate of gold engraved with the words "Holy to the Lord," which Aaron was to wear on his forehead, apparently to help everyone keep their parts straight. My boots came with a tag that read: "Genuine Leather, Ozark Trail." They didn't have any with gold plates. I'll try to remember my part anyway.

These days you can buy all kinds of prayer paraphernalia: crystals, incense, video cassettes of famous pray-ers, audio cassettes of words of power, icons, statues, pictures of Jesus in a startling array of poses, holy bells and whistles, oils and unguents. My hunch is that it's best to travel light, and you could do a lot worse than to get a good pair of boots. Why not do it in remembrance? Maybe we'll meet on the trail.

CHAPTER 3

Fast Relief with Mr. Bricklin
Suffering and Salvation

*A*friend once remarked to me that the reason pastors are so tired around Easter is that they have to preach about something they don't really believe and it just wears them out. Some clergy will tell you their fatigue is due to all the extra services, studies, and observances that cluster around the season. One wonders what it is that calls out the sudden burst of piety and round of religious soirees, if it is not the need to reinforce our sagging faith.

Evelyn Underhill describes spiritual growth as a "series of oscillations between states of pleasure and states of pain which fatigue the immature transcendental powers."[2] Whatever the cause, the amazing truth of Good Friday and Easter is more than most of us can swallow, let alone integrate in such a way that we remain in possession of the power of the Risen Christ while at the same time surrendered to that power. The thought of it is enough to make us want to take a nap.

Death is wearisome. Suffering is wearisome. Evil is wearisome. Evil wears us down, grinds us down. It is monotonous, boring. As the antithesis to creativity, evil employs repetition as one of its weapons. It is the slow, steady accumulation of minor abuses and violations that, over time, turn into an onslaught that erodes our best intentions. Sick and tired of it all, we finally succumb with a yawn and let death have its way with us.

JESUS SAYS, "Come on. Take up your cross and follow me." Jesus doesn't summon us to a quick, easy death. He says "cross"—that slow torment that keeps you hanging around, conscious, gasping, while your body strains and sags against the nails that pin you to your own circumstances and the slow agonizing drag of gravity does its job.

We slowly sink into the earth, the forces of the universe pulverizing us over eons into dust. At such a prospect, heartily endorsed from pulpits far and wide, one's transcendental powers, mature or immature, might well benefit from a swig of Geritol.

"Have a Happy Death," my friend says. And I go read those eccentric saints who extol the joy of suffering and actually prayed to share in Christ's pain. What did they know that I don't know?

A while back I got a large envelop in the mail with the words SECRETS THAT CAN BANISH PAIN emblazoned across the front. Inside a Mr. Mark Bricklin promised to send me secrets that would save my life and show me HUNDREDS OF WAYS TO GET FAST RELIEF. I looked over his offer and decided to take a nap.

Our culture has difficulty understanding anyone who would deliberately seek to suffer. Can you imagine a twelve-step group made up of Saints Paul, John of the Cross, Francis, and Teresa sitting around some church basement smoking cigarettes and drinking coffee? One of them stands up and says, "I am an adult child of God, and I am addicted to suffering."

Is it possible to distinguish between the suffering of sacrificial love and suffering that is meaningless and self-defeating? It is hard for us to believe that suffering consciously chosen and accepted could be anything other than dysfunctional behavior.

This may be part of the reason the season wears us out. This Jesus hanging on a cross for our sakes appears hardly functional. He makes none of the promises of Mr. Mark Bricklin, who exhorts me not to deprive myself and my loved ones of the chance to truly banish pain. "Mail the enclosed card today!" The effort of leaning up against that cross in a culture that seeks to banish pain and the real spiritual work of extending ourselves past our exposed doubt deeper into God is more than a little fatiguing.

Spiritual growth may be seen as slowly deepening belief, or the steady erosion of our hypocrisy. Layers of pretense and self-deceit are peeled away to expose our fear. What is revealed is the limit of our belief, its edges. A good deal of our suffering may be that raw exposure of our doubt, our unbelief, to the light of the Risen Christ. It stings, smarts. We think we are dying, losing everything.

Five-year-old Cicelia asks, "Mom, why did Jesus have to die on the cross?" Yes, why do we have to have Good Friday before Easter? What is the relationship between suffering and salvation?

A friend who is a battered wife remarked to me, "Having Christ in your heart doesn't mean you are a little rug." How can I teach Cicelia the difference

11

between being a little rug and joining with Paul in suffering the loss of all things and becoming like Jesus in his death? (Phil. 3:7–11).

PERHAPS THE DIFFERENCE between tragic suffering and the redemptive suffering in which Christ invites us to participate lies not in the amount, kind, or quality of the pain, nor in its cause. That which makes one kind of suffering sacred and healing and another simply one more case of horror and abuse inflicted upon an innocent victim may lie in our response to the pain we experience when others trespass against us.

And here we must look to Jesus, the pioneer and perfecter, "who for the sake of the joy that was set before him, endured the cross, disregarding its shame" (Heb. 12:1–2). We do not have to love our suffering; we just have to bear it. We take up our crosses. We consciously receive the pain that comes our way, not for the pain we must endure but for the joy that awaits. Then we become martyrs in the best sense of the word. *Martyr* means witness, one who has seen God and is willing to testify by one's life that God lives—even in the midst of death and evil and defeat.

Perhaps what those long-suffering saints know that Mr. Mark Bricklin and I haven't yet grasped is that what makes suffering redemptive is enduring the cross, despising the shame, making light of its disgrace. Unlike Jesus, we do not despise the shamefulness of our suffering; rather, we despise ourselves. We are humiliated and contemptuous of ourselves in situations of disgrace, defeat, and loss, which expose our limits.

We want an explanation for our pain. So we anxiously search for meaning in the mistaken notion that if we understand our pain we may find relief. Jesus does not engage in *what ifs* and *if onlys*. Jesus does not seek to justify himself. His focus is not on the cause of his suffering, but on obedience to the One he loves and from whom he came and to whom he is headed in joyful reunion. Jesus does not despise himself; rather, he despises that which seeks to humiliate and destroy his identity as the holy child of God, in other words, his innate goodness and sanctity. Jesus does not stop loving himself or God in his suffering.

In contrast, when we suffer we often engage in frantic efforts at self-justification, trying to figure out what went wrong where and whose fault it is and how we can prevent this from ever happening again, because we are so ashamed, because we have so much contempt for ourselves.

To be beaten, to be rejected, to be abandoned and despised without beating, rejecting, abandoning, and despising oneself is to know oneself as a child of the Holy One. To suffer, despising the shame, is to remain grounded in one's essential goodness, even when one has reached the limits of one's ability to do good.

CHAPTER 4

Witches and the Easy Yoke
God the Father as the Source of Salvation

*I*n medieval times people planted cedar trees in front of their homes to ward off witches. The witches were believed to get caught in the trees, counting the needles and forgetting why they had come.

I have been caught counting needles lately: "One Ken doll leg, one Barbie head, two tiny plastic hangers, four My Little Ponies, Mr. Potato Man feet, potholder, the cow from the nativity set . . ."

When the children were younger, I discovered that I loved order more than I loved God. Up until then I had been able to account for every item in my household. But eventually I had to get used to gouging my foot on strange objects, peeling odd substances from the carpet, and routinely shouting, "Where are my scissors? Who took the tape?" One Christmas my brother gave our girls a set of plastic toy dishes. He grinned at me as we watched them open the large box containing forty-eight small plates, cups, saucers, salad plates, teapot with lid, knives, forks, and spoons. The one upon whom I had inflicted many atrocities when we were young leaned back against the couch with a satisfied grin. He knew that for the rest of my life I would be pulling tiny forks out of my underwear drawer.

I wonder if archaeologists have turned up evidence of cleanliness-and-order cults competing for the affection of Yahweh. Perhaps this is a modern heresy. I got a cult catalog the other day full of alluring brightly colored boxes of all sizes with labels that can be stuck, glued, snapped, velcroed, and sewn to anything. I ogled at desk trays, cupboard organizers, file cabinets, shoe trees, and gadgets consecrated to bringing order to every room of my house. I longed for the peace they promised.

I do not know how I came to equate the peace of Christ with the order and pristine simplicity of a Zen garden. He was clear in telling us the peace he was leaving is not as the world gives (John 14:27). But I keep getting caught in the needles and forget why I have come to God's house.

Last month we consecrated the hermitage and land as a holy meeting ground for God and whomever God calls here. So now what do we do? What does any individual or community of faith do once they have claimed sacred space, when they finally say with authority and power, "Here, now, this place, this moment, this task is really holy"?

Our minds provide a steady stream of ideas and improvements and developments. One thing after another appears to demand our urgent attention and action. We are tempted to back off and betray the very reality we have invoked. We have found more needles to count. But really, we have no excuse now. There is nothing else to do. It is time to pray.

CICELIA SAYS she wants to be an archeologist and a ballerina. Digging through the sandbox she came across a small white stone she believes to be a dinosaur tooth. Now she wants to dig up the whole backyard looking for "bones and real gold and real silver." She carries her dinosaur's tooth in a tiny tin box with other treasures she calls her "magics." The other day she took apart her bear that sings. "I think there is a magnet inside," she said.

It starts early, this need to dig into the depths to find the magic that dwells beyond what we can grasp here on the surface. It is the holy attribute needed to avoid getting caught in the needles in order to penetrate past the distractions and attractions and obstructions to reach the core. Otherwise, like the witches, we forget why we have come and spend our days sorting through the kids' toy box and grumbling about how messy everything is.

Of course, we need to balance prayer with action, but the action must know its purpose and its source. We can wash the dishes mindfully. We can be attentive to God as we chop wood and carry water. But why do I chop wood in the first place? Does this action, do these words, this shift in me to engage in some purposeful activity for God, rise from my own or another's fear and anxiety? Does my activity come from my inability to tolerate the tension of my freedom in God? Or does it seem to originate from a different place in me?

Such attentiveness to our motives may help purify our intentions. One may begin to notice that some of the time we do the right things for the wrong reasons. A good deal of the time we do the wrong things for the wrong reasons. And once in a while we do the right thing for the right reason.

Action that originates in such righteousness has an eternal quality to it. It is unhurried and full of grace. It flows with economy and precision, purity and power. It is poor, chaste, and obedient. It does not call attention to itself but points beyond to the transcendent reality.

And Jesus has promised us that it is easy and it is light.

IN HIS ASSURANCE that his yoke is easy and his burden is light, Jesus has given us a means of discernment for whether or not our action is moving out from the Source of Love. Does what I am doing feel heavy, dark, difficult, like hard work? Am I enmeshed, entangled, conflicted, in pain? If so, I probably have stuck my neck under the wrong yoke.

The redemptive power of Jesus' life, death, and resurrection lies in his self-identity. He knew who he was and was unwavering in his conviction that he and all he did came from this beginning. He was so clearly and consistently aligned and yoked with this creating source that he himself became the instrument of redemption. And he promised us that such access to redemptive power is ours as well.

In what was for his time a startling choice of image, Jesus named this place from whence he came *my Father*. He recognized what impelled him to creative activity as father, as a masculine parent. Father, who thrusts outward and begets, had thrust him outward into the womb of creation from the immense stillness of the Godhead as active life giving energy in human form. Jesus called Father that which pulses and swells in the heart of reality to reach out, to encounter, to know and be known, to penetrate, and to be received.

This One, whom Jesus introduced to us as Father, extends himself to us in vulnerable longing. Little renders us more vulnerable than the desire to join in loving relationship with another on whose response and cooperation we are dependent. And out of the vulnerability of the need to procreate is born an even greater vulnerability: becoming a parent.

Addressing and contemplating God as Father, however, has fallen on hard times. Important work has been done in lifting up the Mother, the feminine nature of God. And as space is given for God, the Mother, to rise in her fullness, we may find in ourselves the compensatory need to shatter any puny father images we may be carrying. As the feminine is revered, former narrow images of God the Father may be expanded to reveal father as something beyond what we may have thought of as father up to now.

As we examine the intent of our actions, we might ask this question: Do my actions spring from my Father in heaven or my fathers on earth? Is my action yoked to mortal structures, paradigms, expectations, and norms? Or is my action joined to the light, easy yoke of the Source of Life?

Many have been opening to the presence of God as feminine. And we have been simultaneously valuing the feminine principle in ourselves as both men and women. We need to do the same for the masculine principle. Both the feminine and the masculine have been devalued and trivialized by our time.

When we seek our authority in others, in wealth and possessions, in physical or intellectual prowess, instead of in God the Father, we will be continually defending and protecting this authority and threatening any who might question it. When our authority comes from God, we respect and value our power to bless and to curse. We do not use words carelessly. We make sober, wise judgments and take responsibility for the power to create and beget and parent that which has been entrusted to us.

Jesus' yoke is easy and his burden is light. What is not easy for us is the radical restructuring, the free suppleness and flexibility of mind, body, and spirit that is needed for us to submit to and keep our necks in Christ's yoke. It is nothing less than a revolt, as far as the lesser fathers and mothers in us and around us are concerned. To them it feels like death, a sickening restructuring of the fundamental organizing principle of our being. They taunt us with the question asked over and over of Jesus: "Just who do you think you are anyway?"

Under the light and easy yoke, we are free and detached from the need to please others or to obtain particular results from our actions. Jesus' yoke calls us into ever deepening trust in our begetting source and in our identity as holy sons and daughters of God.

HOLY GROUND can be seen as the fecund human soul—feminine, waiting, receiving, eternally offering itself for the sheer joy, ever fruitful—the matrix of divine and human encounter. But this holy ground finds its balance, its joy and deepest fulfillment, in that ongoing procreative activity with its Father, who has heard the cries of his children suffering in Egypt and has equipped us through his Son to be redeemers. To make holy ground is to be a mother; to be a redeemer is to be a father. We have been called as individuals and in community to be both.

CHAPTER 5

Lunch Boxes
and the End of Summer
The Tension of Poverty and Abundance

The leaves of the pear tree outside my study window at home are glossy and thick. The pears, a bit larger than walnuts, blush rose near their stems. On my window frame hangs an icon of a skinny, naked Jesus. This Jesus will not meet my gaze but looks down some hellish tunnel of sorrow that hallows the space between us. His face is gray, mouth turned down. He is wearing a sheer loincloth that looks like it came from Frederick's of Hollywood. I am embarrassed for him in his poverty, his utter abasement. Cheer up, Jesus! You look terrible. The pear tree is laden with fruit this year!

Jesus doesn't seem to notice the fruit, though he must see it—his eyes are wide open. Pinned like a specimen to the cross where under his arms are gathered stately mourners, he bleeds in tiny spurts from hands and feet. Angels hover over his head in neat rows. One appears to be performing a liturgical dance. No—that's no angel. It must be Christ on his way to heaven, ascending in a crimson mandala.

The crucified Jesus just hangs there. Has he no shame? It is I who squirm, not he. For his eyes pin me at the intersection of poverty and abundance, where I hang ripening in the Kansas sun in late July. O Jesus, how long must you hang there suspended in misery, wearing us out with that sorrowful stare?

With an introit of barking dog, the squirrels soon will come to pluck the half-ripe pears with their agile paws, taking one bite from each and then carelessly tossing the rest to the ground to rot. Pray God to preserve us from squirrels that raid at dawn, chattering and chasing up and down the branches, tempting us into thinking that we have been made to be consumed by squirrels. Pray God that we may be left hanging, suspended by the heart's stem, hidden in the leaves until we've ripened properly. And then, at the sharp insistent teeth of need, open our flesh, sweet and tender, to one another.

Then maybe that sad Jesus will get off that rugged cross and come eat the fruit of summer with us.

WE WENT TO KOGER'S Variety Store for back-to-school specials the other day and painstakingly put names on new backpacks, glue bottles, scissors, and Big Chief Tablets. We watched Dad's jaw drop as he wrote the check for new clothes at the mall. Then last evening we noted it was getting dark so early.

The air is uneasy, a mix of the eager hope of a brand new lunch box and the painful regret that summer is over and we never got around to making those doll clothes or camping out in the backyard to watch the stars all night.

JEREMIAH LAMENTS with us, "The harvest is past, the summer is ended and we are not saved" (8:20). And we find ourselves at the intersection of poverty and abundance where the kingdom of God is conceived. Christians seem to perpetually stand on the threshold of a new school year clutching our shiny lunch boxes in one hand and the forsaken dreams of summer in the other. Holy ground is the paradoxical place where we simultaneously live in the Pentecost fullness of the gifts of the Spirit and the power of the Risen One and in the crucifixion emptiness and cry for redemption of the Suffering One.

Jesus tells us that of God's own will we have been brought forth to be a kind of first fruits of God's creatures. Like the firstborn child or the firstborn of livestock, the first fruits to come ripe in a season were sacred to God. "But when the grain is ripe, at once [the farmer] goes in with his sickle, because the harvest has come," says Jesus (Mark 4:29). When one is ready to die, then harvest is come. How odd to be ripening for death, to be growing in Christ only to be handed over.

Just as the cross is the joining of two opposite directions, we live in the creative tension of the union of poverty and abundance. The tension is great, and it is hard for us to stay in the center of the cross for very long. We want resolution. We are tempted to heave ourselves down one polarity or the other. But if we can hold both the pear tree laden with fruit and our ongoing need to be nourished, if we can accommodate both the Risen Christ and the Crucified Savior, then we may discover, out of the union of these opposites, new fruit conceived in us that will heal and sustain the earth.

The barrage of demands and the voracious appetite of a culture that seeks to devour rather than savor its sustenance undermine a quiet, patient trust in God's seasons of growth and harvest. What is it that finally brings us to fruition? Is it not the sharp insistent teeth of need, our own poverty and the poverty of one another, that finally allows us to fall, sweet and tender into each other's embrace?

AT TOYS R US—Toys are us! In Proverbs, Wisdom tells us, "At the beginning I was playing beside him like a little child and I was daily his delight"[3]— I listened to a tinkling recording of "It's a Small World, Isn't It?" while a lion and a lamb, a giraffe, a hopping kangaroo, and a waving bear shimmered across a plastic screen. Nearby, Cicelia plinked a xylophone in plunking delight.

"Are shoes alive?" she later asked in a department store.

"No!" exclaimed her older sister.

But Cicelia persisted, "I saw one talking on TV."

"Let's see," I said, and leaning over a cordovan Bass loafer inquired, "Are you alive?"

"Oh, Mom," Diana sighed.

We tried on grownup perfume. When the saleslady offered to help we told her we were searching for a fragrance that was really "us." A spray, and Cicelia pressing her hands to her cheeks giggled, "Oh, Mom, I know this one is me!"

Before boarding the escalator, we tried on hats. Cicelia, in a large-brimmed red felt with ribbons, and Diana, in a small black veiled cloche, gazed at their images in the narrow mirror on the best day of my life.

We took six dresses from a rack for Diana to choose from. Cicelia was her handmaiden letting it be according to her word—carrying, doing buttons and zippers, and holding up the blue satin fabric like a swatch of heaven against each dress.

JESUS, I THOUGHT you were suffering, but I saw streams of light pouring from your head, like a fountain, spraying colors—blue, azure, hues of red, green, yellow—shimmering rainbows irradiating in spurts and gushes and rivers from a still, small body sagging on a tree. All day I played plinking magic while you spun streams of green leaves, jungles, hay fields in spring, purple hyacinths, beets, cerulean seas, dolphins, berries, mountain mist, and a single red-rose flame out of the chaste and tender aureole of your pain. There in the dance of creation and dissolution, there where our need is met with the abundance of another and our abundance fills another's lack, there where it is a small world after all—there is our joy made complete.

PART II

. . .

Tell the People That I Miss Them

*T*he more I prayed, the more sensitive I grew to the suffering of others. I became acutely aware of both the presence of God and the presence of sin and evil. The violence of television made me ill, and the morning newspaper left me in tears. I began getting migraine headaches. I became oddly sensitive to people, cities, electronic gadgets, and florescent lights. I wanted only to be very still and silent.

Talking, teaching, and being around people became more and more difficult. Speaking about God as an object seemed like rude gossip, while God was so intensely present to me. It was an effort to shut down my awareness of God's presence enough to objectify God in reading and teaching. Why talk about God, when we could be with God?

The world was charged with an inexpressible beauty and sanctity. A tenderness so fine and pure that it made all the love I had ever known before seem coarse and vulgar held me in its sweet embrace. Something as ordinary as the rocker in my living room brought me to my knees in tears one morning with a sense of the awesome journey of the molecules that made up its polished surface.

At the same time, much of the world seemed alien, and I often felt painfully out of place. Polite conversation seemed like meaningless babble. Why couldn't I be like other people? I wondered. What was wrong with me? The culture, including the Church, was stampeding past the beauty and holiness in all that God had made. We seemed liked bulls mindlessly grazing in a china shop, continually stepping on and squashing the exquisite sanctity of one another.

Then one spring I spoke to a group of churchwomen in Sabetha, Kansas. I had a practice of asking Christ what I should tell the people before I spoke or preached. For years I had heard, "Tell the people that I love them." This time as I was being introduced, I asked my usual question, "What do you want me to tell the people?" *Tell the people that I miss them*, the voice replied.

Later I dreamed someone was weeping. I heard deep anguished sobs. I awoke confused and called out in alarm to my daughter, "Cicelia?" Silence. Then, "Who is it?" I asked. "Jesus," the voice replied.

This poignant loneliness of God and divine longing for our companionship became the heart of my understanding of God. God was vulnerable—and God's vulnerability rose out of God's passionate love for us.

My compassion for the suffering Christ and identification with him through my pain deepened. I became angry and impatient with anyone who did not share this sense. Jesus was becoming the focus of meaning and purpose in my life. I worried that I was becoming a fundamentalist, and struggled to find words and images to articulate for our time what I was coming to understand that God is accomplishing in Jesus. One Holy Week I slept little and wrote in a white heat about Jesus and redemption, as I tried both to resist and to reconcile myself to the intense interior conversion of my soul.

Late 1990–1992

CHAPTER 6

A Voice Crying in the Pasture
Redemption

*T*he wind has been blowing since yesterday. It is blowing, blowing down all the ways, sweeping in gusts, lifting and shaking us. The new moon is at hand.

The children take big trash bags out on the lawn and, holding them out behind them, run in circles—"to catch some wind," they say. When they come in breathless, cheeks red, puffing and laughing, I ask, "Where's your wind?"

"Oh, we let it go."

There is a great stirring, a bold reordering afoot. All night the wind roars round the hermitage, praying in gusts and creaks and groans, tossing branches and sticks and rattling pods.

A wild-eyed figure in camel's hair strides over the pasture making a straight path toward us. "Repent!" he hollers over the wind. Wielding an ax, he peers at us, measuring our fruit, scrutinizing our roots. Repent? Who, us? Why, we just want to get along.

The compassionate love of God, though boundless and ever present, is received in its redemptive fullness by the broken and contrite heart. We can hardly be saved unless we know we are lost. Yet, at a recent church gathering a friend noted that there were many prayers offered for intercession, petition, and thanksgiving, but few of repentance.

How does this happen, this redemption, for which the creation groans and heaves itself in wailing blasts and tempests? How do we participate in the healing of others, of the earth? In the Christmas story God shows us how.

Redemption describes a particular kind of relationship with reality. The Hebrew term for "redeem" means literally *next of kin*, a close relative, part of the family. A redeemer is one who engages in responsible saving action on behalf of another known as an intimate relative.

A redemptive relationship with all that surrounds us is a relationship of loving intimacy. Intimacy is that willingness given us by God and shared by God to be with what is foreign on its terms without forfeiting one's own distinction. This is one way to describe the Incarnation. In Jesus Christ God is being intimate with us.

As the story tells, God so loved the lost, the world, *what is*—that God became what God loved so that the ones who believed in this love should live always in the presence of the Source of Love.

Redemption is loving what is lost enough to become it, loving it enough to give one's holy child, the essence of one's being—the self—to the beloved. The heart of redemption is not knowing, but loving. And it is not our technique and reason that save us, but our passion.

Could we relinquish our grip on our own identities long enough to become the poor, the homeless, the AIDS sufferer, the refugee, the abandoned child, the man on death row, even the polluted and defiled earth? Is it possible to let go of our precious self and become anyone, anything that stands before us?

We die to ourselves and for another that there might be space in our being to be filled by that other. God died the first time when the Holy Child sprang from God's heart and nested in a young girl's womb. And the space in God was filled with the world. God died the second time when the Holy Child of humanity gave itself up on the cross. And the space in humanity was filled with God.

You want to give a gift? You want to redeem, heal, and free others? Love them. Love them enough to give them what is most precious to you—your only holy child, the most beautiful and pure part of yourself. Give them your child knowing full well they will be unable to receive it with all the reverence and love it deserves.

In giving yourself, your sacred self, you become filled with that which you love. You embody the beloved. And the world rushes in on the wind to be swaddled in holiness and to be redeemed.

And the voice of the one crying in the pasture borne on the currents of the earth's grief is heard and obeyed.

CHAPTER 7

The Rejected God
Gnosticism

*R*ecall a time when you gave yourself in love to another—a time when your heart opened and you offered your being in radical trust and joyful self-giving. Such loving is the free, frank need and lusty thirst of an infant at its mother's breast, the tender vulnerability of a child displaying a new drawing, the hazardous unveiling to stand naked in your imperfection before the eyes of another.

Remember how you wanted to pour yourself out for this one and how the more you allowed yourself to love, the more of yourself you discovered. Remember how the world ignited in glory and you with it. How you became braver, happier, more beautiful and alive. And remember, too, how love poured through you, blessing those around you as it flowed toward your beloved.

Now perhaps this object of your love betrayed you, for sometimes mortal lovers prove false. If you were betrayed, can you remember your shock, humiliation, rage, and the suffering that pierced and impaled you and pinned you like a dumb animal to a torture rack slowly turned by ruthless unfeeling powers?

That pain which takes you to your darkest night, which crushes you under your greatest fear and reduces you to meat as a victim of the cruelest abuse, that pain is a portion, your portion, of the suffering of your Lord Jesus Christ.

"Are you able to drink the cup that I drink?" he asked. To have given all one has out of love and to have suffered rejection is to drink Christ's cup and taste with him some of the immense suffering of this God who risked everything for us in radical vulnerable love.

Charles Williams wrote that we would never find what is true unless we have given our whole heart to that which ultimately must prove false.[4]

To have loved and lost is to have been chosen and prepared to find the treasure that will never leave or betray us.

THE LENTEN SEASON invites us to examine our betrayals, our hidden contempt and shame for our lover Jesus, and to see more clearly how deeply we have hurt him. In some places Jesus has fallen on hard times—nothing new to him, of course. He remains as much a scandal and folly today, as much an object of shame and manipulation in this century as in the first. Who wants a God who fails, who looks like nobody special, who says, "Come follow me and suffer"?

Each age has its idols and many hearts give them sanctuary. One of these idols is Gnosticism. Gnosticism asserts that by intelligent knowledge of the arrangement of the universe we will be able to map out our own way of salvation. Such a notion invalidates and betrays the costly redemptive work of Jesus Christ. This perennial heresy first appeared in the Garden when we fell for the line that one bite would insure knowledge and make us like God.

The Gnostic in us may know a lot about how to know God, about spiritual gimmicks and doctrines, rites and rituals, but what the Gnostic in us does not know is Jesus in his fullness.

Paul writes in Philippians:

> I regard everything as loss because of the surpassing value of knowing Christ Jesus, my Lord. For his sake I have suffered the loss of all things, and I regard them as rubbish, in order that I may gain Christ and be found in him, not having a righteousness of my own that comes from the law, but that comes through faith in Jesus Christ, the righteousness from God based on faith. (3:8–9)

The fact is that the better we know Jesus the more deliberately we will cling to him as our only salvation.

Currently a busy spiritual bazaar is serving up foolishness and poison to hungry, wounded folks who, in one way or another, have been turned off by the Church and traditional forms and are willing to settle for superstition, mumbo jumbo, and the spiritual equivalent of junk food and toxic waste. This is a grave fraud and, in some instances, dangerous. It is also a rejection of Jesus.

Sorry Jesus, you embarrass us. Of course I believe in you, but you see my path is nature spirits. I am sure you'll understand in this post-Christian, neopagan era.

Sorry Jesus, I would rather tune in to a spirit entity, go to my transchannel, read my cards, hunt for a vision.

Sorry Jesus, but you see I am a feminist and your Church turns me off.

Sorry Jesus, but I just can't stand the way the evangelicals or the liberals or the fundamentalists or the Catholics or the Baptists or the Presbyterians talk about you, and I have decided to let their image of you determine my own, so I need to go bow before something else that doesn't make me so uncomfortable.

MOST SECULAR psycho-spirituality is silent regarding Jesus. The current attraction to new-age or old-age esoteric exotica may partly be resistance to grace and hostility to Jesus Christ. In some cases, in what appears to be benign philosophical and spiritual advice resides an unspoken enmity to Jesus that is demonic.

Some seek to protect a violated earth and her creatures, while ignoring the power and completeness of divine revelation in the defiled Child of God who hung on a cross. We tend to our inner child and seek healing for our wounds, yet we continue in our steadfast refusal to receive this Child of God in his deep vulnerability and love for us. It is a measure of how neglected we all are, I suppose, that we are so blind to the neglect we engage in on a cosmic level.

Four hundred years ago, while actively engaged with enemies of Christ in a period of church reform, St. John of the Cross wrote in *The Ascent of Mount Carmel*:

> Any person questioning God or desiring some vision or revelation would not only be guilty of foolish behavior but also of offending God, by not fixing his eyes entirely upon Christ and by living with the desire for some other novelty.
>
> God could respond as follows: I have already told you all things in my Word, my son, and if I have no other word, what answer or revelation can I now make that would surpass this?

> Fasten your eyes on Him alone, because in Him I have spoken
> and revealed all, and in Him you shall discover even more than
> you ask for and desire. You are making an appeal for locutions
> and revelations that are incomplete, but if you turn your eyes
> to Him you will find them complete. For He is my entire locu-
> tion and response, vision and revelation, which I have already
> spoken, manifested, and revealed to you, by giving Him to
> you as brother, companion, master, ransom and reward . . .
> Hear him because I have neither more faith to reveal nor
> truths to manifest.[5]

Could this neglect, hostility, and shame for Jesus be a mirror of our own
hidden hostility and contempt for the incarnate reality of ourselves? To love
Jesus and find in him, and him alone, the fullness and completion of God's
revelation is to receive ourselves with the same trust and grace. As I am
embarrassed by, doubtful of, or unmoved by the reality of Jesus Christ, I may
also be embarrassed by, doubtful of, or unmoved by the reality of divine
truth residing in me. To reject Jesus or to engage in spiritual adultery by
being seduced by cultural and religious Gnosticism may be to reject oneself
in one's deepest vulnerability and radical risking love.

Perhaps we are recapitulating the whole history of human spirituality in
our current explorations in order to reestablish ourselves more deeply in
truth. Simone Weil wrote that "Christ likes us to prefer truth to him, because
before being Christ, he is truth. If one turns aside from him to go toward the
truth, one will not go far before falling into his arms."[6] So we remythologize
the tired old mundane church-school Jesus and that out-of-date Father God
and the wily, undependable Spirit into a new language and symbol system,
into a new myth that does carry power, does mediate numinously redemption and love.

We groove on Shekinah, Sophia, Shiva. We hunt the logos in the I
Ching, tarot cards, enneagram, and personality type. We call down mystery
with chant and drum. We seek truth in our inner being. We chart our
dreams and strive to become differentiated, individuated beings, until
SMACK SLAM BANG we splat ourselves up against that truth and discover
that truth is Yahweh, *I Am Who I Am*, and I Am is nobody's fool and everybody's Jesus Christ.

CHAPTER 8

Playing Dress Up
Pretense and True Belief

This is my body, peeled back, broken open for you. In my palm blazed Suchness, a torn fragrant crust of What is So.

O common One, you are so plain, so familiar, so simple that we miss you in our desire for some other novelty. We seek you in mystery, ritual, knowledge, magic—all the things we hope will take away our pain and imperfection. We think that if we can just become enlightened, then we will be one with you. And here you are, hurrying toward us, loving us so much, brokenhearted, risking everything to be with us in our unenlightenment.

Jesus, you are things as they are. Here is where I meet you in quiet splendor and completion. Over and over as I bump up against imperfection, resistance, fear, there you are, grinning at me, sanctifying the moment, redeeming in streaming satin rivers of grace what is so.

*P*aula's School of Dance put on a recital last month, and most of Holton as well as a good portion of the heavenly hosts turned out for it. I think God's heart goes out to the dancers and the dreamers who are bold enough to reach for something they are not, because the capacity to imagine and conceive promise, yet unborn, is the foundation of faith.

A good place to watch this happen is on a hot evening in a high school auditorium full of proud parents sitting transfixed, amazed, and delighted by their own young progeny. We know that's no mermaid up there. It's Jenny Mitchell from over in Centerville; her mom works at the bank. But for three minutes Jenny has become a mermaid, and because of her belief we can all breathe under water.

When the dancer becomes the dance, the veil lifts. When the pray-er becomes the prayer, when nothing separates us from God—no self to comment, evaluate, compare—then the forms of prayer drop away and the heavenly hosts arrive packing picnic lunches and lawn chairs and settle in to watch the show.

Someone ought to open a School of True Belief where we could learn how to believe until there was nothing in us that was not a believer. Every June we could put on a recital. There we would solo in some show-stopping number where we would cease watching what we are doing and just do it in the free spontaneous expression of our souls' passion.

True believers are rare these days. To know nothing but Christ and him crucified, to be wholly available to God as God desires, we must be full of faith in the context of the essential truths of our life.

We cannot in the end be pretending about what is real, and yet pretending can help us learn. It may even be a necessary step on the journey. Pretending may be evidence of both our unbelief and our devotion. Through the gift of the ability to make believe, we can imagine and try out what is unimaginable. And our response to our own and others' pretense ought not to be condemnation but encouragement of deepening belief and trust in the power and reality of whatever pretending we are doing.

Eventually, having discovered truth itself, we will no longer cling to the external forms. They will appear shallow and pretentious in the face of the deeper reality they have encouraged us to discover and take hold of in ourselves. And when at last we find truth and truth finds us, then we may need to forgive in ourselves and in others that which we have found false. We can both expose pretense for what it is and invite others through make-believe to *true believe*.

The foundation of spiritual growth and theological hope lies in the ability to risk what doesn't make sense or seem possible. A lot of the time we look like kids traipsing around in Mom's high heels and old prom dress. We smear on lipstick and crouch in the tree house being famous ice-skating stars and novelists. We giggle and sip Kool Aid from the stemmed goblets we lifted from the kitchen. Our pretending doesn't last very long, though; pretty soon

Karen's little brother will come around and throw tomatoes at us. But we are practicing the fine and awesome art of becoming our dearest dreams.

Someday we will find ourselves on some holy ground—a mountain, standing before a kitchen sink, tucking a child into bed—still practicing, still trying out the deepest desire of all: to know and be known by the Holy One. We will read up on how to do it. We will take classes. We will listen to ones reputed to be in the know. And we will pretend a lot. Then that day, who knows when or how, grace will strike us. And we will know that it is all true. And the game will be over. We will be home. And we will never have to pretend again.

And all the rules we made up when we were pretending will seem silly and useless. Like how you are supposed to eat your chips in your sack lunch first and save the gummy bears for last. How if you get home before your sister after school that means Dad will take us out for a Dairy Queen after supper. How if you pray this way or believe that or wear this totem or light this candle, things will turn out okay.

And then the very powerlessness and need of childhood that drove us to pretending in the first place, the very unacceptability of ordinary being, that tender vulnerability at the mercy of powers greater than us, and all that we did to impose sense and order—then that unfinished irredeemable self becomes the holy ground of redemption.

I remember the wild longing of age ten when I sat in the sun eating purple grapes, warm and sweet, spitting out the seeds at my brother. Summer was interminable and nothing ever happened except the daily routine of my hopelessly mundane family and Andy Griffith reruns. That longing took me to the cool dim corridors of the public library, hunting ecstasy. I would haul home stacks of Nancy Drew mysteries and *American Girl* magazines and read about other times and places where Nancy motored about the countryside in her roadster, where something more interesting than hanging out the wash and canning chili sauce was always happening.

Can we share in the wonder and deep need of the Great Pretenders? Can we cherish our vulnerability and say, "Go for it, pretend your hearts out! Go on. You be the Goddess of the Moon and I'll be the Wise King. The back porch is our kingdom and the dogs can be our ladies-in-waiting. Here, you can walk on water and I'll heal the sick. Pretend and dress up and play until your dreams come true."

This is how dreams come true. One day when you are playing, your ladies-in-waiting suddenly bolt, trailing their old-curtain gowns across the lawn to chase a squirrel. One day the Moon Goddess gets a mean streak and scribbles crayon all over your royal decrees. One day your cardboard castle disintegrates in a sudden rain and your whole kingdom washes away. On a day like that, when all your pretending is exposed and you are just a little kid filled with an ache for bliss you cannot name, then someone like a mother or a father will come to you and pick you up and wipe your nose and tell you that you are beautiful just the way you are. And the wild hunger to be known and honored and loved for the holy child you are is at last met by the Holy Child of God.

I DO NOT KNOW if our pretense amuses or offends God. I do know there is a time for us to stop pretending about what is not and bless what is. For when I stop acting out my fantasies and stay here to drink this cup poured out and eat the bread of this moment, then I meet Jesus, the One who came and keeps on coming into the world just the way it is, not to condemn it, but that it might be saved through him.

CHAPTER 9

Holy Cows
Evil and the Wilderness

*O*ut in the wilderness there is little time for contemplation. Everything is busy eating or being eaten. An ant drags a cookie crumb across the floor. The spider battalion stands guard at sticky mines strung all over the back porch. The iridescent hummingbird hovers near the feeder. All day grasshoppers ping against the screen and land with a thump to chomp most everything. A daddy longlegs cruises up the side of my cup and tastes my tea with a delicate finger.

"Eat my body," Christ says. And, "Feed my sheep."

"How am I able to give them meat to eat in this wilderness?" asks Moses of the Holy One. And God sends quail.

And the quail come here, eighteen of them, weaving in a line through the tall grass with their low gurgling chatter, to forage under the willows along the shore. The quail also need to eat.

I get hungry, too. I just spent forty days in the wilderness, and I have learned that the wilderness and hunger go hand in hand.

IMMEDIATELY AFTER JESUS is baptized, God sends him out into the wilderness. The Greek word for "wilderness" refers to abandonment. The wilderness is an arid wasteland, a lonely place where the wild beasts dwell, the demoniac wanders, and many dangers assault the body and soul.

For Jesus, the wilderness is the place where nothing separates him from God. Here is the resting place to which he calls his disciples to come away. For me, the wilderness is the perilous place where—out of our conviction that it is our availability to Christ rather than to the world that will bring in the kingdom—we become more available to God than to one another.

In the wilderness we contend with powers and principalities, with forces of evil on many levels. Evil rarely shows itself on the face of anything. It permeates and veils—and it comforts. It encourages us to persevere in the habits and attitudes that deny Christ. Evil is seductive and seeks to satisfy appetites. It does not confront. It shows up when we are weak and lonely. It promises great things it cannot, will not deliver. It lies.

The spiritual awakening of our time presents a formidable threat to the powers of darkness. Therefore we may expect spiritual pursuits to be more subject to attack and perversion than are other human undertakings. There is, after all, more at stake here. When the presence of satanic cult activity in a small Midwestern town makes the newspapers, there is a whiff of Armageddon in the air. What constitutes protection in this battle is more than a wave of smudge stick or a perfunctory prayer of confession on Sunday morning.

What is needed to bring clarity and purity to our powers of discernment is not likely to be found in either a vision quest up a mountainside or in a beefed-up vacation church school. We do not so much need new curriculum, new translations, new rituals for worship, or new myths and oracles as we need deeper, more radical appropriation of what we have already received. We need to penetrate the deceit and evil in our hearts and institutions, peel away corruption and illusion, and hold ourselves open before the searing light of Christ.

Satan tempts with form, the manifestation of spirit in the world. "Here, turn stones to bread. Throw yourself down and be saved. Worship me and you will have all the kingdoms of the world." None of these—bread, salvation, or the kingdoms of the world—are evil in themselves; all are part of God's good creation. The evil enters in the manipulation and abuse of form for one's own ends as one satisfies one's hungers and thereby worships self over God.

A problem with spiritual pursuits is that we bring to the forms our addictions. We pray to become better addicts. We seek power, prestige, health, wholeness. Here our prayer is a function of our disease, our attachment to creation. Then spirituality becomes akin to aerobics, jogging, health food—something to do that will make us more attractive and successful. We approach spirituality for what it will do for us, not for what it will do for God.

I came to the wilderness in part because I heard Jesus crying and saying he was lonely for us. I came out of a growing sense of God's hunger and need for us and for one who would stay with him one hour. I came to discover how it would be to delight in and enjoy God for God, not for what God could do for the world or me.

And I found along with my brother, Simon Peter, that the spirit is willing but the flesh is weak. And to pray with Christ is more difficult than praying to Christ.

Are there some among us who are willing to watch with Christ one hour? Are there some willing to turn in radical belief and trust toward God and away from the forces within and without that seek to deny Christ?

Is there one willing to pay the cost of staying one hour, of tasting and knowing God's suffering in her bones, of being bereft of all mortal assistance, of contending with a near constant onslaught of devils, of serving as bridge between heaven and earth and thereby, bearing in her body, mind, and psyche both the immaculate tenderness and the surging ferocity of divine love and the immense ocean of mortal sorrow?

Like Peter, I couldn't do it. For along with my good intentions I brought my weariness and poverty and dependence on God's mercy. And my eyes grew heavy, and I slept.

But God slept, too. Christ rested, too. For Christ brought to the wilderness the same as I: weariness and poverty and dependence on mercy. And so, like two homeless children huddled in an alley, like two lovers entwined, we slept while the owl hooted and the bullfrogs boomed and the little gray mouse nibbled bread in the corner.

THERE ARE A LOT OF COWS out in the wilderness where I stayed. These are hungry cows. Their main job in life is to grow big and beefy, and they approach their calling with a single-minded devotion that puts me to shame. I spent a good deal of time chasing them off the several acres around the cabin, separated from the rest of the pasture by a split-rail fence.

In a drought, the stone foundation holding the gate leading into the area around the hermitage, which I called holy ground, split and fell apart. Various designs of baling wire failed to deter the cows. Once I rigged up some yellow rope and a latch hook to fasten the gate. I was sure this would keep them out. For two days a large Angus grazed with a bright yellow rope garland round her neck, until she finally managed to ditch it.

This Angus had an eye for the succulent grass down by the lake in front of the hermitage. One morning I awoke and found her gazing at me through the window. She stopped chewing and took to her heels when our eyes met. But the black madonna and her son began to make regular visits and soon had several holy cows in their company.

One evening I held church out in the pasture by the cottonwood tree. I quoted Scripture, preached about not trespassing, sang a hymn and, searching for a bovine language, spoke in tongues. The next day they broke through the fence again.

So that is how the black madonna, her son, and the only saved cows in Jackson County, Kansas, came to holy ground. It was their hunger of course that did it.

Surely, God knows all this and likely considers the compost pile in your backyard as much of a holy spot as anywhere else. God mercifully draws us into divine union through our addictions and sin. Hungry seekers drawn to shrines and sacred mountains realize what any authentic holy spot makes immediately evident: the strife is over, the battle won.

Yet it is to Satan's advantage that we continue in the dark about this. That is why all human method, doctrine, ritual, or anything in the created order must always be weighed and sifted to make visible its innate impurity, which generally amounts to some version of denying the salvific work of God already accomplished in Jesus Christ.

Our God-given hunger and thirst draw us to greener pastures. There are no fences around Christ's kingdom. Everyone is invited to sit down at the feast.

CHAPTER 10

Urgent Mother and Child
Holy Indifference
and the Repose of the Virgin

*O*nce a friend took me to visit her holy space in Syracuse, New York. I was teaching a workshop on sexual abuse and spirituality. About forty-five persons had gathered to tell stories which were excruciatingly painful and yet all too familiar. We concluded the day with a service of healing and holy Communion. Tired and yet exhilarated, I was aware of the pain of Christ at the violation of these holy children of God. I was also grateful to have a small part in reconsecrating the dwelling of God within each person.

My friend came up to me afterward and asked if I had the time for her to show me something she wanted me to see. After such intense intercessory work, I needed adoration, some hushed stable where I could kneel in shafts of silence. I went with my friend.

We drove downtown and hurried across a plaza in the fading light to a side entrance to the Cathedral of the Immaculate Conception. My friend led me up a few steps and around a corner to a tiny chapel big enough for only two kneelers.

And there was the Virgin Mother waiting for us. Sculpted by a woman artist, the larger-than-life bronze statue filled the small space with love. Seated with her hands palms up on her lap, the Holy Mother embodied both all pervading compassion and perfect repose.

> *Hail Holy Queen enthroned above.*
> *Hail Mother of Mercy and of Love, O Maria.*
> *Here, receive these ones, these violated virgins,*
> *desecrated altars, these bruised, abused, and broken ones.*
> *They are yours.*

And swiftly, cleanly, the outrage and grief I felt was drawn out of me. Here was God as the Mother of Mercy and Love, attracting and receiving like a powerful magnet the suffering I carried. I rose to my feet aware of the pain but in no way oppressed by it. For a long time I had known the compassion of God. At last I met the repose.

> From the days of John the Baptist until now, the kingdom of
> heaven has suffered violence and the violent take it by force.
> — MATTHEW 11:12

DURING THE ADVENT season, we read the apocalyptic Scriptures about the Second Coming of Christ that speak of great upheavals, wars, distress, and terrors of many kinds. We may wonder why redemption is greeted with such turmoil. The spiritual awakening in our world today is paralleled by ever escalating violence. What is there about the advent of God that occasions such chaos?

Mortality resists its redemption. The coming of holiness must confront that which seeks to violate it. The darkness comes to holy ground because it wants to be redeemed. But as Jesus suggests, people of violence do not know how to take the kingdom without force.

Perhaps this is because there is very little in the created order that is pure and virgin enough to house holiness without violating it. The response of creation to the incarnation of the uncreated is jealousy, rage, and desire. It covets and it grabs. Out of its own ancient history of abuse, it lusts after what it has lost, and attempts to steal what has been stolen from it.

Pure merciful love can feel like acid to an abused creation. It burns and stings like an antiseptic on open wounds. The earth flails and pulls away, howls and lashes out in its pain. The preachers exhort, "Believe, believe and you will be healed," while the sick planet knows instinctively that true belief will increase its pain. Better persist in numbing denial and bitterness and grab what you can from whomever you can, than expose your wounds to the burning rain of grace which lances sin and cleanses with Fuller's soap.

WHO IS IT, what is it that can stand between the holiness of the Coming Christ and the violent upheaval of creation resisting its redemption? What can possibly be strong and true enough to hold both the suffering, broken world and the Holy Child of God and not be torn apart by either? The Virgin Mother. Even the name we use speaks to the paradox of emptiness and fullness held in the image of Mary.

Meister Eckhart wrote that a virgin is someone who is free of all false images and is detached toward God's dearest wish and ready to fulfill it unceasingly, as was Jesus.

The original sense of the word "virgin" is a person who is one in him- or herself. Such a person is free from possession and possessiveness and is capable of the total giving of self, body as well as soul. The virgin aspect is that which is unpenetrated, unowned by humanity. It does not need to be validated or approved by anyone to know its own innate worth.

Virgin carries much of the same intent as the word for "holy," which means *set apart, the temple*. The Parthenon (literally, "the virgin's place") was the temple to Athena on the Acropolis in Athens. In the New Testament *virgin* is used to depict the host of the redeemed in Revelation and to refer to the community as the bride of Christ. But by far the most frequent use of the word *virgin* is in the Bible's figurative description of cities, nations, and communities. We often find *virgin daughter* as an expression for Jerusalem.

THE VIRGIN IS ONE who can hear and believe the anguished truth of a violated and profaned creation. The virgin does not indulge in denial or false hope. She has no illusions about the extent of the horror and suffering we inflict on one another. The virgin refuses to protect the perpetrator.

At the same time, the virgin refuses to protect the Savior. She is at once Madonna and Pieta. For she possesses a holy detachment, a divine indifference, which preserves her purity and allows her to receive the suffering of the world and pass it on to Christ without being abused by it.

Holy indifference is a rootedness in the truth and abiding goodness of the unseen while trusting in the unfolding of the seen without interfering or forcing the seen to accommodate itself to me on my terms. The virgin remains intact, whole, and in possession of her divine identity, while at the same time offering herself to the ravages of profanation. Her only pain is the grief of further wounding her beloved by offering to him the abused of the world.

For the virgin knows that it is not our empathy that heals, not our outrage that heals, not our grief that heals. It is our *faith*—our trust in the power of Goodness to prevail over darkness. The virgin does not respond to suffering and sin out of her own anxiety and fear and wounds but, rather, out of her repose, her absolute serene trust in the One she carries in her womb and continuously delivers into the world. Such as she are the healers among us.

41

MY SMALL DAUGHTER, playing with the figures in the wooden stable, sings her lullaby: "Round yon urgent mother and child, holy infant so tender and wild."

This mother, more urgent than virgin, smiles: Yes, Holy Infant, tender and wild, you are so wild, so undomesticated, and so radically other than anything known and familiar. No matter how hard we coax, you will not eat out of our hands but remain out in the timber hidden in the brush. We set out bait, offerings on the snow. Cowboy theologians toss ropes into the forest and lasso decoys. And roughrider ecclesiastics try to corral you in sedate doctrines.

The virgin daughter of Jerusalem sings at the gate. In the dark we lay a trail of breadcrumbs to our door. We wait, stilled, hushed. *Come, Lord Jesus.*

But who can stand when you appear? The earth shudders, mountains topple, creatures shiver with fear. Shots ring out in the forest. Innocence awakens and moves toward us and the rough hand grasps for its lost treasure.

THE VIRGIN DAUGHTER of Jerusalem stands on the path, and suddenly she is falling, falling into the blue sea, into the wide sky, falling through pain and fear and despair. She falls faster and faster, plummeting like a stone. She plunges through a tunnel formed at the intersection of the cross hairs in the telescopic sight aimed at redemption, where opposites meet and all things come together.

She whizzes down the tunnel like a child's slide, sleek and silent, silver in the sun, falling free. And the kingdom does not suffer violence. And she is not taken by force. And the two, who have been made for each other, delight to have found ground holy enough to hold each other's purity, ground strong enough to bear each other's pain. And in her joy she funnels greatness from the wideness of her hope down the narrow passage of her being into us.

So now I pray for passionate virgins who have died for love and dwell beyond the clutch and fever of desire. I pray for eccentric virgins who live on the outskirts of propriety and raise geese and talk to trees. I pray for violated virgins and their reconsecration. I pray for virgins who find the courage to reject the lie that eats away their souls and whispers that what happened never happened and leads them down a winding path of mirages and fun house mirrors that mock truth.

I pray for virgins who find the courage to reject the voice that hisses the blasphemy that someone is making all this up: "Not only was there no sin, but also no angel ever came. There were no wings, no light nor presence, no glory and no peace. And that voice you heard, that spacious cloak that wrapped you round, the comfort that was given, will be as unremembered as the terror."

I pray for virgins who know they are only as holy as they are willing to see how horribly they have been profaned and how horribly they profane. I pray for priestly virgins who preside at their own sacraments, who ordain themselves to love, who anoint and purify. I pray for virgins who refuse to bypass pain but, in their surrender to it and annihilation, fall into the center of their humility to sit enthroned in the trust of total repose and divine indifference from which all healing flows.

I pray for virgins, calm and pure, to stable holiness and for virgins, safe and gentle and true enough, to conceive the immaculate tenderness without doing it violence. I pray for undomesticated virgins, unpenetrated by conventional values, virgins unconfined by reason and impervious to demands of fathers and mothers.

I pray for revolutionary virgins who despise the shame and take up the suffering for the joy that awaits. I pray for virgins whose land, enclosed by strength, is untouched and guarded by a flaming sword. I pray for virgins who, with unveiled eyes, gaze unflinchingly at evil and at God and live to tell the tale. I pray for virgin martyrs who are witnesses with the conviction to believe their own eyes. I pray for chaste, intrepid, impeccable virgins incapable of doubt.

I PRAY FOR VIRGINS who apply themselves to prayer until their souls become clear, focused lenses through which we spy the intricate dazzling structures of divinity enlarged for us. And God, hidden in the forest, is magnified by them. And glory sprints across the clearing, kicking up a cloud of blessing.

I pray for virgins who are not afraid of greatness, either the greatness of themselves or the greatness of God. And I pray for a virgin with a heart that dilates. I pray for a bold virgin who—when she has grown as big as she can be, when she has come to the outer reaches of her being and all that she thinks and knows and hums to herself—will give up encompassing plentitude. I pray for a virgin who becomes emptiness, who will fling herself like crumbs in a fragrant trail from what was once her heart to the forest, and who will say: Let it be to me according to your word.

And the shy, tender God takes the bait. And she and holiness are won. And their Child tumbles wet and wild into the wounded world to heal us with his stripes.

CHAPTER 11

Prayer as Subversive Activity
The Good Service of Adoration

*A*n unnamed woman comes to Jesus in adoration and does a beautiful thing. The Gospels of Matthew and Mark tell her story (Luke and John, too, with some variation). To onlookers, her adoration seems wasteful and extravagant. They shake their heads in dismay, "How can she spend all her energy, all her love, all her money on that! What a waste. She would do better to sell her resources and give the money to the poor."

Jesus halts their judgment, "Wait. Do not trouble her. She has done a beautiful thing. You will always have the needs of the world. You will not always have me before you—the immediate lucid presence of God incarnate. She has done what she could. She has anointed my body for burying beforehand. And truly where the gospel is preached in the whole world, what she has done will be told in memory of her." With these words this woman's act wins higher praise from Jesus than any other recorded in the New Testament.

Jesus calls the woman's action "a beautiful thing." Another translation renders this as "a good service," neatly reconciling the false dichotomy between contemplation and action. Here contemplation, the prayer of adoration, is understood as action and work of the highest order.

When is the last time you did a beautiful thing? Can you recall a time when you poured yourself out in reckless adoring love for another, a time when you squandered your resources and sacrificed what was most precious to you? What does it mean for you to adore? How do you handle the rebukes of onlookers? What is your flask of costly perfume?

The Church is long on edification but sometimes short on adoration. We do not encourage or give opportunities to ourselves for much adoration. Adoration, the spontaneous selfless expression of love for God, is our highest end and the task for which we have been created, according to the

Westminster catechism.[7] Adoration in Hebrew means literally the act of bringing the hand or fingers to the lips in praise. Biblical forms of adoration include removing the shoes, bending the knees, prostration, kissing. Laying the hand upon the mouth implied the highest degree of reverence and submission.

How is it to behold what is before you and lift and move your hand through space and past all else that cries for its touch and put it to your mouth?

I remember as a child standing rapt with my hands pressed against my mouth gazing in adoration at the most beautiful baby doll I had ever seen. It was in the department store where my father worked. The doll was actually a mannequin used to display infant wear, and it sat in perfection on a high shelf. I longed for that doll. Every time I went to the store I went over to the infants' and children's department and stood in awe at the feet of that rosy-cheeked creation. I felt awakened in me passion, desire, love, the longing to give myself completely to something, and the anguish of unfulfillment.

Much of the poetry of St. John of the Cross speaks of the beauty of God and the prayer of adoration. Carried away by love, he wrote the first five stanzas of his poem on mystical union, *The Spiritual Canticle.* In the fifth stanza John, in the pursuit of his beloved, writes:

> Pouring out a thousand graces
> He passed these groves in haste;
> And having looked at them,
> with his image alone,
> clothed them in beauty.[8]

GOD INVITES US to adoration through the created order, which is imprinted with the beauty of the creator. And we, smitten by a love that is ultimately inexpressible, do what we can. Given the reality of being housed in this mortal flesh and held in time and space and the vicissitudes of our life situations, we do what we can, not the fullest expression of our adoration, which will always be limited in this life. But for now we do what we can, which is to anoint beforehand the body of our love for burial.

Adoration is doing what we can in the face of life's transient nature. All that we adore in creation will pass away. It will fail us. It will not be what we had hoped or dreamed. It will be somehow unattainable.

So we pour out what is most precious to us on the One who stands before us, saying: *Oh my dearest one, you, too, shall die. Here, this moment of grace as I gaze in your eyes, my little daughter—here, this graceful sway of the branch of river willow yellow-dappled in the sun—here, this sip of hot tea warming my throat—here, my friend, in your exquisite perfection.*

All will suffer. All will pass away. So I break out of myself and the needs of my world, to run to Simon's house to find you and lose myself, as I perform the act for which I was created. I break open my heart and pour the sweet fragrant oil of my love upon you.

SUCH GOOD SERVICE is radical revolutionary activity. It may not get the dishes done and the annual report written. Adoration subverts the little fathers and mothers within us and without as we set our hearts to be about our Father's business. If the disciples, those closest to Jesus, object, it is little wonder that we must endure the harassment of internal and external indignation.

Yet what awaits one who adores Christ is delight, refreshment, fulfillment, and participation in the redemption of creation. The need to grasp and clutch at experience, possessions, relationships, dissolves in the presence of the All in All. Adoration gives birth to freedom, the freedom to let things be as they are. We do not need to demand that the world be a certain way for us, because we are no longer attempting to extract from the world what only Christ can give. And because all of creation reflects the beauty of Christ, we care for one another with utmost reverence and tender regard.

Finally, adoration purifies the soul. Simone Weil wrote that each minute of attention to Christ actually destroys a part of the evil we carry.[9] The longer we gaze at the perfect purity of Christ and expose our souls and the souls of all those we carry in our hearts to the beauty of God in our prayer of adoration, the more redemption flows through us to heal creation.

IT IS NOT MONEY that will ultimately feed the poor, but the radical, subversive, good, and beautiful service of adoration. And that is why the kingdom will come not when the hungry are fed but, rather, when "at the name of Jesus every knee shall bend in heaven and on earth and under the earth and every tongue confess that Jesus Christ is Lord."

PART III

· · ·

A Spirit of Judgment and a Spirit of Burning

On that day the branch of the Lord shall be beautiful and glorious, and the fruit of the land shall be the pride and glory of the survivors of Israel. Whoever is left in Zion and remains in Jerusalem will be called holy, everyone who has been recorded for life in Jerusalem, once the Lord has washed away the filth of the daughters of Zion and cleansed the bloodstains of Jerusalem from its midst by a spirit of judgment and by a spirit of burning.

—ISAIAH 4:2–4

*N*ot everyone I met on Turtle Street gave sound directions for the way home. I came across a few blind guides and ignorant teachers. One inadequately trained and unethical religious professional misled and exploited me, and this experience compromised my health, leading to several years of medical care.

Exploitation requires a certain unwariness in the victim. In my case, I turned a deaf ear to the voice of truth and wisdom sounding the alarm in my own heart. As my eyes eventually opened to the injury and negligence of my teacher, I came to appreciate the wrath of God and God as judge.

As I slowly regained my health, the love of Christ illuminated deeper levels of my being. Time passed. One day I came to the sobering awareness that I had been a spiritual prick. As I walked out to the car after spending a day at the hermitage, this precise appraisal struck me like lightning. The sudden vision of my pride and egotism grounded me, just as an electrical charge leaps from the heavens to converge with its opposite in the earth. The disillusionment and loss I had experienced cracked my false self and put me in touch with a self more real, more free, and more grounded than I had been before. Facing into the sin of others and my own sin required me to come to terms with not only the injustice in my life and in the world but also my guilt and responsibility for the way things are.

A recurring question for me has been, What difference will my praying make to the poorest person on earth? I felt a responsibility to my suffering brothers and sisters on this planet. What right had I to indulge in stillness and solitude, hidden away in a pasture, while others were bent double under the weight of injustice and poverty?

I began to see that few had any desire to pray in such a way as I, and that since God had given me the desire I ought to exercise it. I even wondered if perhaps the universe was counting on my being faithful to the person God had made me, even as I count on the pear tree being true to itself and not suddenly sprouting feathers and dropping ripe roosters from its boughs in September.

In Jesus, God made holy the unique and specific. It is possible that we become redeemers as we are faithful to that which is strange, peculiar, and rare in ourselves. So I offered my prayer on behalf of others who do not know how to pray or have the time or inclination to do it. I often did not know for whom I was praying. An immense will and overwhelming love flowed through me into the world. I seemed to be merely the channel—an available soul opened both to God and to creation in love—through which the earth's need moved into God and God's mercy flowed into the earth.

1992–1993

CHAPTER 12

Sacrificial Suffering
A Channel for the Urgent Love of God

*My sheep hear my voice. I know them, and they follow me. I give them
eternal life, and they will never perish. No one will snatch them out of
my hand. What my Father has given me is greater than all else, and no
one can snatch it out of the Father's hand. The Father and I are one.*
—JOHN 10:27-29

We know a good deal about tragic suffering, the kind of senseless suffering that diminishes us individually and corporately.
I think we know less about sacrificial suffering, the suffering
that becomes a sacrifice is freely, consciously chosen or accepted on behalf of
others out of great love.

Jesus said greater love has no one than to lay down one's life for one's
friends. Sacrificial suffering is the path of downward mobility, the deliber-
ate turning away from the voracious, never-satisfied voices of an addictive
consumer culture toward finding one's security in what is eternal and
imperishable.

When we follow Jesus, we find the way to true sacrificial suffering which
brings redemption and healing. And it is the sheep—those who have recognized his voice and believe—who are asked and equipped to make the sacrifice: to generously share our wealth, to offer prayers of repentance and sup-
plication, to confess our guilt and responsibility for the way things are, and
to undergo personal hardship, self-denial, loss, and suffering on behalf of our
brothers and sisters on this planet. True prayer convicts us of our complicity,
our intimate involvement in the oppression of others. None of our hands
are clean.

We will not discern the shepherd's voice by being conformed to the world. A transformation is required, a renewing of our mind, a reconstitution of the structures of knowing and naming and experiencing reality.

Sacrificial suffering is born out of love and intimacy with creator and creation. It is freely chosen. It means intense struggle with the forces of evil. It means pain. It means loss and deprivation. Sacrificial suffering is rooted and grounded in the eternal, what is imperishable. Witnesses from various religious traditions remind us of the need for such radical love.

Rabbi Moshe Lieb of Sassov taught that one who could not with equanimity suck the puss from another's wound had not yet come to understand the power of God's love. He said he learned that "to love means to know what the other lacks."[10]

Teresa of Ávila wrote that she didn't believe anyone who claimed union and yet remained always in a state of peaceful beatitude. Such a union to her mind involves great sorrow for the sin and pain of the world, a sense of identity not only with God but also with all souls, and a great longing to redeem and heal.[11]

Baron Von Hugel wrote to his niece that he wondered whether she realized "a deep great fact—that souls, all human souls, are inter-connected, that we cannot only pray for each other, but suffer for each other. Nothing is more real than this inter-connection, this precious power put by God into the very heart of our infirmities."[12]

"God enabled me to agonize in prayer," writes David Brainard. "My soul was drawn out very much for the world. I grasped for a multitude of souls."

And Evelyn Underhill observed, "As [the] personality [of the saints] grew in strength and expanded in adoration, so they were drawn on to desperate and heroic wrestling for souls; . . . that redeeming prayer by which human spirits are called to work for God."[13] Underhill's awareness of the costs of vulnerable involvement with others in intercessory prayer led her to write to her spiritual director that she did not think she was strong enough yet for this kind of prayer.

Many persons are praying these days. A cry of outrage and pain is being raised to the heavens all around the world. Yet, I have an odd sense that God is helpless to respond without us. God anguishes to see the people of the earth and her creatures so racked with poverty and violence, but the way God can respond to these cries for help and healing is to inspire human beings to be channels of grace.

To be a channel we have to be open at both ends, both polarities of our being—the human and the divine, or the mortal and the eternal dimensions. What pokes the holes in us is our suffering, suffering freely received and consciously offered—just as when Christ was penetrated by evil, his wounds became passages for redemption.

Jesus wears his wounds in the resurrection appearance stories. They are not miraculously healed. The Risen Christ in the world is the Wounded Christ in the world. And the Risen Christ in you and me is also the Wounded Holy Child in us—who is choosing to offer his or her wounds for the healing of others.

Strangely, the suffering of others heals us. This is the truth the prophet Isaiah was pointing to when he wrote of the Suffering Servant whose stripes would heal us. The Servant is bruised for our iniquities and bears the chastisement that makes us whole. The purpose of God's people, the covenant community, is to become such suffering servants who bear simultaneously the scars of God's judgment upon sinful humans and God's merciful love.

Yet we may be ashamed of and embarrassed by our wounds. We may think our pain means there is something wrong with us, something we better get fixed or repaired or replaced. Or we may think our pain means there is something wrong with someone else—someone we need to impose our will on in some way. But maybe there is nothing wrong with our pain. Maybe there is something wrong with our minds and how we think about our pain. Maybe our minds can be transformed in such a way as to understand that the hardship of the human condition is merely God poking holes in us for the love to flow. And the more we resist the struggle and suffering, the harder it is for God to act powerfully in the world.

Such an understanding does not diminish the suffering we encounter or alleviate our sense of abandonment and desolation, but it does have a vision of the future that includes eternity. It knows that there is something more at stake here than what I can see and hear and name or snatch, and it is willing to live its life out of that reality on behalf of those who do not recognize the shepherd.

For the world to change for the good, we need not so much a new political direction as a willingness to wear our wounds without shame and allow them to serve God and creation as apertures of grace.

Christians are called to be transformed persons who live on intimate terms with God in freedom and largeness of spirit. In the face of evil, instead of blaming and attacking and beating, Christians allow themselves to be pierced through by evil, following the shepherd all the way to the cross and becoming channels for the urgent love of God on behalf of all people.

CHAPTER 13

Playing Barbies
Life after Enlightenment

Overheard in upstairs hall:

"You be Ken. I'll be the wife. Let's say we have three children and one is an orphan. The wife's name is Samantha Parkington; no, let's make it Sonora. Now the ball is tomorrow. Say it is next morning and this is a very nice dress she always wears. Pretend the prince comes.

"Hullo, Prince," in sultry voice.

"Hullo, Princess," in husky male voice, "I have dreamed galore!"

"Pretend they are circus stars and they do tricks on this rope. Barbie likes to wear this pink outfit for their act, or should she wear one of her bikinis?"

"Now lower them down," whispered.

"Wait. Mom'll get mad. She's got somebody down there."

"No she won't. She'll never see."

"Here they come, the Great Zambinis!"

"Hee, hee, hee."

The summer began with a trained-dog act on the front porch featuring Sarah, our twelve-year-old hound. Her main tricks were sitting, shaking hands, jumping over a stick, and lying down (after her mistresses sat on her). Although the tricks were few, Sarah's costumes were not. For her first act she wore a red net tutu with satin cape and red bows in her ears. She segued into act two in a yellow leotard, followed by an orange-and-purple sequined number for the finale (lying down) that showed off her haunches to great advantage.

Then there was the elegant Victorian tea party featuring ice cubes with strawberries inside, bingo, Old Maid, and perfumed wrist corsages. We had a puppet play with puppets made of Styrofoam balls stuck on Popsicle sticks. The original drama was about two fairies who go to a magic store and meet a bad witch who puts a spell on them. Both fairies spoke in high-pitched fairy voices, so it was difficult to understand them; and the witch forgot most of her lines and kept getting the giggles. Just the same, the parents and neighbors who turned out for the show applauded in all the right places.

For a time the backyard tree house was a ship in search of pirates and treasure. There were hours of dressing up. One day the children were rainforest dwellers, wearing head wraps and sarongs and dragging out all the stuffed animals. There were bike rides and swimming and drawing class and fights over the hammock, and when one didn't know what else to do, there was always playing Barbies.

Each day, when a playmate went home, when tempers flared, when someone wouldn't share, or when a game just came to its natural conclusion, there came that sudden brutal question: Well what next? And the girls would hunt me up and announce with great anguish: "Mom, we're bored. There is nothing to do!" My suggestion list—practice piano, read a book, or help fold laundry—just served to increase the pitch and volume of the whine. Next came the tactic that my mother passed down to me: "Oh run on outside and get the stink blown off you." In the end, they settled in contentedly playing Barbies.

Playing Barbies, of course, is one of the prime activities of little girls between infancy and puberty. It serves as a transition from here to there when you do not know what else to do. First, over the years, you collect as many Barbies and Kens and Skippers as your mother will allow. You gather up scraps of cloth and papers and countless tiny plastic things like coat hangers and shoes and sunglasses, and you keep them in a box that is too small, so that several Ken and Barbie body parts are always dangling over the edge.

Then you find a place to spread out. Under the dining room table is good. Before the TV is ideal. Outside is okay, but you always have to lug all the stuff back in at the end of the day. The best place is in the upstairs hall alcove that overlooks the stairs. Mom will let you keep the Barbie stuff spread out there for up to two weeks before you have to pick it up because the cleaning lady is coming.

Next you have to decide what kind of Barbies to play: Cinderella Barbies, Peter Pan Barbies (where everyone will fight over who gets to be Wendy), Ken-and-Barbie-get-married-and-adopt-an-orphan Barbies, Barbie gets kidnapped, Barbie goes to college . . .

Then you have to decide who plays what part, and then set things up. For Ken-and-Barbie-circus-stars, you have to find some string to lower the Great Zambinis on. A featured segment of their act is dangling over the railing by an arm or leg to turn in daredevil circles in the living room below while Mom is entertaining guests.

I HAVE FOUND a new word. I read it in a couple of newspaper columns. I heard it one morning on the radio. Then two friends used it in the same week. The word is *segue*, a verb, as in "We will just segue from the main course into the peach cobbler and homemade ice cream" or "After that number we can segue into the last piece and the closing song."

I had to look it up. Musicians know "segue" as a term that means literally *to follow*; it directs the performer to continue without a break into the next section. But the word only recently made its way into my consciousness in Kansas. "Segue" certainly sounds more interesting than just to keep going.

I recommend it. I have never been very good at transitions, those nasty intervals between what is and what is about to come, where anxiety haunts and desire licks her lips. I whine and protest, just like my daughters. But a segue makes those awkward transitions almost as smooth as playing Barbies.

A WHILE BACK I asked Jesus what is going on in contemporary spirituality with all this proliferation of spiritual gadgets and interest and the appreciation and retrieval of ancient nonchristian forms. What does the appeal of spirituality mean in the context of the decline in influence and numbers of mainline Christianity? Well, all he said was, "The fat lady hasn't sung yet."

The fat lady hasn't sung yet. Yes, it is not over until it is over. Meanwhile, we hesitate with eager groaning in the transition, looking for something to ease the anxiety of living in the tension of the present moment.

What happens when you have just put on the best puppet show in the whole world and everyone has gone home? What happens when your eyes are full of light, when your mind has shared the mind of God, when your heart breaks with compassion for the planet and her suffering? What happens after enlightenment, after Christ appears to you and you fall on your face in the dirt? What happens then? Do we wait for direction from on high: "Segue into Second Coming"?

Like those who have had near-death experiences, we are faced with the transitional question: Given what I now know and have seen and believe, how will I live my life?

"Mom, I don't get it. I just don't get it," Diana says like some startled creature suddenly yanked from its natural element and plunked down in a foreign place. "Sometimes I think I must be dreaming all this, or that maybe I am just a little mouse in a corner somewhere watching myself."

I STOP ON OUR WAY to the garage, stepping over the wagon. Well, yes, who are we anyway? I wonder. And where have we come from? I suspect the world is a whole lot wilder and more incomprehensible than any of us can imagine.

We admire a smooth execution, a nicely done presentation. *Segue* connotes a picture of graceful ease into the next phase. A friend likes to speak of making graceful passages and transitions. Well, it would be nice, I think, as I trip over the roller skate next to the wagon, but my transitions seem to come in jerky fits and starts, in headstrong, impulsive acts of grandiosity and fearful hiatuses of inertia.

More likely we are yanked up from the road to Damascus, as cantankerous as ever, and holler witlessly, "Hey, what's going on? Who turned out the lights? What happened? Who's in charge here?"

"Since I could not see because of the brightness of that light, those who were with me took my hand and led me to Damascus," tells Paul (Acts 22:11). Paul's segue took at least three years; and even after that, it appears that a good deal of him was left swooning on that road, attempting to bridge the awesome chasm between heaven and earth.

I USED TO SAY pretentiously that my goal in life was to drink a cup of tea well—mindfully, in a state of beatific gratitude. Now I am aware that such a feat is far beyond my feeble powers. And that is why I love Jesus so much. I throw caution to the winds, lift my cup spilling it all over, and slurp the brew running down my jowls.

There is an edge of terror in this enterprise of prayer, and it has to do with the transitions, getting on and off holy ground. A while back, I heard we could build a space station large enough for ten thousand people, but once anyone went there they could never return to earth. Gravity would crush them. In a way, becoming accustomed to the gravity of God leaves us gasping and reeling in mortal gravity. It worries me sometimes how blithely we segue from worship to lunch, oblivious to our peril. If we are half-awake, it seems to me, that passage ought nearly to kill us.

On my way out to the hermitage one morning, I stopped at the grocery store to buy some fruit. The store's early morning activity, the cashier with her red fingernails, the smell of fresh-baked rolls and cookies, the rows of cantaloupe and watermelon, and the aisles of canned vegetables comforted me. It was all so normal. No one here spent hours on bended knees. No one here was so reckless as to dare to negotiate with God. I felt like a crazed hermit, a madwoman reeling from "encounters of the third kind," finding solace in the predictable certainty of Ron's IGA.

"Why don't you go home, trim the grass and finish your planting, weed the flowers, do the laundry?" I asked myself. "Go home and take hold of some solid task that has a beginning and an end, the sort of task the neighbors can see and nod approval of or you can show off to your friends?"

GOD DOES NOT photograph well, and prayer does not lend itself to ledger books. The alpine climber swings over the crevasse in solitary daring and plants a flag on the summit with only the wind and glacier to witness. He returns, sunburned, breathless. "I saw," he says; "I saw it all."

"I am what I am," God says. God knows the divine Self for its own sake, not in relation to anything else. I shudder to know myself in that bold, barren way. "I am . . . , " I say and hunt over and over for something, the right thing, anything, to drive my stake in a small crack where I can dig my fingers in and hang on as I dangle over the universe by virtue of my own strength.

Instead, I am dangled with Ken and Barbie Zambini. Attached by the thin string of my unique being to the Holy Child, I circle in the brightness of that light. And I secretly chuckle with delight at how my witness startles the sedate folks in the living room and in Corinth, Ephesus, and Muncie, Indiana.

CHAPTER 14

Persimmons
Justice and the Wrath of God

*T*he new moon dangles the evening star, like a silver spider on an unseen thread, and perches in the black branch above my head. A brown leaf loosens itself and falls like a sigh. And persimmons pepper the sky.

It is the time of year when time is running out. Time is running down, picking up speed. The earth is tipping over and everything is pouring like grains of wheat into the winnowing basket. And slumbering prophets wake wild-eyed and stomp across the land and holler that even now, even now the ax is lying at the root of the trees.

Once when I was a child my mother gave me an unripe persimmon. When I bit down on it, my stunned lips shrunk, my shocked gums drew back from my teeth, and the soft, innocent skin of my mouth cringed at the acerbic taste of the unpalatable fruit. "You need to know how this tastes," she said.

"Why?" I asked, shaken to be fed a thing so foul.

"So later you will know," she answered.

"CAN YOU DRINK THIS CUP?" asked Jesus. "It will be bitter to your stomach, but sweet as honey in your mouth," the angel told John when he took the scroll and ate it (Mark 10:38; Rev. 10:9).

DARE I EAT A PERSIMMON? When the thin stream of smoke from the supper fires carries the aroma of soup and muffins and the sky is charcoal lined with scribbled branches, I walk around the lake carrying seeds in my pocket. One persimmon had four; the other had none. I hold the wrinkled fruit in my mouth and taste the translucent green of spring and the soft violet of summer nights heavy with crickets and stars.

"Yes, Lord, we can drink it." But the fruit turns and galls us. Our mouth grows fur, and the wrath begs to be spewed out. "Let it be to me according to your word," she said (Luke 1:38). Blessed are you, Daughter of Zion. For now you will carry God's wrath in the wizened fruit of your womb. And Simeon will tell the young mother, "A sword will pierce your own soul too" (Luke 2:35).

"You brood of vipers," the prophet howls. "Who warned you to flee from the wrath to come?" (Matt. 3:7).

Look up ahead. The Child who redeems horror is coming our way. The perpetrators will inflict their rage, their sorrow and dead dreams on his perfect body, feasting on his immaculate tenderness like voracious beasts.

The fruit hung still in the trees like dark ornaments. You waited for a long time, stomaching bitterness. O Lord of Hosts, how many trips did we make around the little lake, season after season, until you could tell us how much you hurt, how sad you were, and how we were responsible for your pain?

YOU NEVER THOUGHT we would believe your word. And you were right. We believed the words of this world. We knew how to read the signs of the weather, but we could not read the signs of the times.

A child wept in the night. Someone stalked holiness, waiting in the weeds to pounce on purity. "Who do you say that I am, turning in your womb, hunched and beaten?" you asked us. "I wore your pain and rage like a second skin, a bitter rind, while I mellowed in the long cold night, slowly turning bitterness to sweetness, wrath to salvation. I, suspended like a pale persimmon, am the immediate redemptive presence, compelling and complete."

The leaves drop away and the truth stands stark and strong. Bare arms stretch out for justice. Something turns in the bowels of God, something swallowed and long tolerated but not digested. Impaled on a cross of suffering, the sad flesh tells the tale we would not speak of.

The cup of wrath drunk for love of us lurches, rumbles, rises from the heart of desecration. The rough prophet staggers under the bowl and bears it to us. "Now that the leaves are gone, now that you can see, can see what you have done—bear fruit worthy of repentance, you evil and adulterous generation!"

THE CATALOGS FILLED with morphine fall on the porch like autumn leaves. Sing us a quiet Christmas lullaby. Pass the eggnog.

I went to a bookstore full of things about Jesus: pastel china plates and racks of cards with butterflies and words of comfort, pieces of wood carved with praying hands, rows of cassettes—and everyone smiled a plastic sort of smile. They boasted fifty-seven kinds of Bibles and little statues of happy children caught in precious moments.

I went to another store that had nothing about Jesus. There was a sign that said Waunita was available to read my palm. They had incense, crystal balls, statues of fairies and wizards, and fifty-seven kinds of Bibles.

Later at the movie theater the woman brought her hand down again and again upon the child, slamming him against the floor. Huddled in the hell of the restroom stall, the child screamed in terror. "Is that all you are going do?" the woman raged. "Let go of my neck," the boy whimpered.

In the car, the solemn children spoke wisdom beyond their years in shaken voices. "Mom, I bet I know why that woman did that . . . because someone did that to her once. Yes, and that little boy is going to do that to someone else someday."

Is THERE A BALM, is there a remedy that can break the grip of hell around our hearts that freezes our souls into anesthetized defense and visits our sins upon our children and their children?

Behold the desolating sacrilege standing in the holy place! Oh the holiness defiled, the violation that revolts the heavens and disgusts the soul.

Go get your higher power. Master the technology of consciousness. Find your inner guides. Meditate until you feel nothing but the spaces. But the violated child in the restroom will meet you in an alley someday, because holiness demands justice and justice demands accountability and accountability leads to repentance and a contrite heart.

What we fail to see is that a god without wrath is the devil. For wrath is a distinguishing feature of holiness. Satan appears as an angel of light, but only true holiness can know itself profaned. Only truth can suffer from a lie. Only goodness grieves the loss of purity.

Unto us a Child is born. Unto us a Child is given. The Sweet Innocence of Virtue Incarnate descends into our hearts to writhe while we inflict our rage upon one another. The Child suffers our sins against it and offers itself for our salvation. But the Child cannot redeem without repentance.

Will the Child pluck evil and pin it against the wall and speak the truth? Will the Child shake sin in its teeth and hold it accountable to holiness?

The Child remains sagging against the cross until the creation says it is sorry. Repentance sets us free from Satan's jaw and the beast that targets joy, gulps down hope, and gnaws away our souls.

GO AHEAD. Pick a persimmon. Hold it soft in your palm. Lift it to your teeth. Pierce the waxy vernix. Feel the pulp like sweet mush and taste the rush of summer mornings and the sound of geese honking over head.

Then wait for your gums to grow fur. Wait for bitterness to spread across your tongue and rankle like a prophecy and lift you by the collar to spit out truth. This astringent fruit, eaten too soon, will mortify and coat your mouth with wormwood to haunt you for years with the taste of regret.

> *O sweet Jesus, O Fountain of divine sweetness, O Joy of our desiring, the quality of your presence pervades the universe like perfume, but you are no precious moment painted in pastels with chubby cheeks, nor are you some slick course in magic where I can insure my own prosperity and unending happiness.*
>
> *Instead, a wrathful moment, you rise out of the throat of the child in the stall on a scream and lift him into oblivion. He will forget. He will forget and be able to go home and eat his supper and watch TV. He will forget and go to school and learn to write in cursive.*

But we must not forget. We must not. And somehow he will manage. And maybe there will be angels who come and maybe not, but the taste of Jesus without justice is not Jesus. And the Child's appalling grief and terror are chilling testimony to the Word made flesh, every bit as convincing as the triumphant cry of herald angels.

The Child, held down, pinned, and defiled, looks into the dull stuporous eyes of evil. And the hate and shame of the creation is left on his perfect body like a foul smear that soaks in and becomes one with him. And his insides turn to mush. And he can only hang from the branch of the tree and wait for vindication, praying: "Bite into Jesus. Bite into me."

ONE NIGHT I FOUND several persimmons on the ground. I didn't have to climb the ditch and stretch to pluck one from a branch. That night they lay right at my feet in the road. And this time they were perfect, wholly sweet without a trace of bitterness, sweeter also than honey and drippings.

Ho! Come and taste the fruit of salvation.[14] Blessed is the fruit. And blessed are you. Hail, Holy Mother. Now I know.

CHAPTER 15

Humpty Dumpty Had a Great Fall
Original Sin

*T*he end of magic is a painful thing. The house lights abruptly go up. We rub our eyes and stumble to our feet, startled to find ourselves inhabiting heavy bodies. Waking from some enchanted evening, we reel dazed into the world looking for our true love.

We had long been in the business of magic. We knew sleight of hand, prestidigitation, illusion. Something was always up our sleeve. And when we saw that it was good for food, a delight to the eyes, and desirable because it made one wise (Gen. 3:6), in one swift move, with a hand quicker than the eye, we reached and grasped and bit into the fruit.

"And all the king's horses and all the king's men" could not put magic together again. And we stood on the outside looking in, as the fiery sword of the cherubim waved wrath in every direction. Then our eyes were opened, and we knew that we were naked (Gen. 3:7). And God came and clothed our vulnerability with soft fur suits.

After the magic has died and lies like gray ash in the hearth, after reality drops her gown and stands brazenly before you with her sagging breasts and stretch marks, after you have given up hope and innocence has fled and you know you are naked—after all that, there where magic ends, is where mercy begins.

And They Knew They Were Naked

The fall from Paradise is a fall from illusion, magic, and glamour. Glamour originally meant enchantment, magic spell or charm, mysterious elusive fascination or allure. Glamour is the delusive enticement that leads us away from obedience and toward satisfaction of the individual will.

Diana was about three when she saw a stranger approaching and jubilantly exclaimed, "I bet he is bringing me a present!" The age of magic is premised on an infantile and narcissistic trust that the universe is cooperating to bring me good and to satisfy my wishes and desires. The age of magic is the time when I expect miracles, and God always seems to be unfolding things so I may prosper. My immediate world and I appear to be immune to sin and evil.

Such thinking is not simply a Pollyanna attitude, nor is it shallow. It may embrace suffering, yet it is founded on the naive belief that if I am good and kind and conform to the line of hope spun out by whatever ideology or theology I may embrace, good things will eventually come to me.

The age of magic perpetuates our tolerance of outrage and evil by our need to maintain our false images of self and God. We say to ourselves: If God is real and active in my life, then this bad thing shouldn't be happening. At that point defensive dissociation may set in, and we may deny what we are experiencing. Or, on the other hand, we may face into the evil saying something like: I have prayed and sought God's guidance. I have been good. If this is happening, then God must want it to happen, and I just need to figure out the lesson here and accept this. Because to allow the converse—that God is not in favor of this, that this offends God and is wrong—is to say that no matter how righteous I am, I cannot control events and insure my protection simply by my own efforts to be good.

As our illusionary trust in our ability to control God and events is unveiled, we fall from the wall of glory and self-aggrandizement into shattering death and hell. Youthful idealism meets mature realism.

This is the harrowing shift in world view from Anne Frank's "In spite of everything, I really believe that people are basically good at heart" to John Calvin's conviction of the total depravity of humankind. Calvin wrote that sin is not our nature, but its derangement: "Being quite content with our own righteousness, wisdom and virtue, we flatter ourselves most sweetly, and fancy ourselves all but demigods. . . . Original sin, therefore, seems to be a hereditary depravity and corruption of our nature, diffused into all parts of the soul."[15]

When we have a great fall, what is being worked on at a very deep level is the painful conversion of our basic instinct to survive, the surrender of the individual will, no matter how holy its desires may appear to be.

And God Clothes Their Vulnerability
with Soft Fur Garments

By the waters of Babylon there we sat down and wept when we remembered Zion. How shall we sing the Lord's song in a foreign land? (Psalm 137).

O God of seeing, after we have swallowed the knowledge of good and evil and our eyes are opened, how can we sing your song? When the scales have dropped away, when the clay has been washed off, when we put on the soft garments of grace you made for us, we stumble dazzled by the light. We who love darkness more than you, tie on blindfolds to simulate the night.

Wayfaring strangers, we wander here in these soft skins, exiles on earth, yearning for a better country. We had bit down and tasted, chewed and swallowed the fruit. Our eyes were opened, and we had seen. We had witnessed something that we could not speak of, yet must tell. We really weren't absolutely sure what it was we had seen, but we thought most of the time that it was God. It is true we asked for it, prayed for it—to see God and live, that is. Perhaps it would have been better to die. Perhaps there are very good reasons why persons who see God rarely live to tell the tale. For now how could we sing a song in this strange land—this earth where gravity weighed hearts to the soil; and mind lay flattened between the pages of time?

What happens if you do not sing? What happens if your eyes are blinded by the light, and it all unfolds before you? What happens if you know the Lord's song by heart yet do not sing it? Does it rankle in your soul, turn sour, spoil, and grow soft, mossy mold? Does it take on a parasitic life of its own, feeding on your body, stealing your joy, eating up your hope?

WHEN HAGAR FLED from Sarah's abuse after she had conceived with Abraham, the Lord found her by a spring of water in the wilderness. God told her she was with child and would bear a son who shall be called Ishmael. So Hagar called the name of the Lord who spoke to her, "Thou art a God of Seeing"; for she said, "Have I really seen God and remained alive after seeing him?" (Gen. 16). Therefore the well was called Beer-lahai-roi, the well of the living one who sees me.

Diana, fifteen years ago when you were born, they brought you, with swollen eyelids and wrapped tight in the swaddling cloths, for the first feeding. When I put your mouth to me, you shuddered. For two days you shuddered as I held you, as one exposed to a chill or to some horror. "Lambie pie," I called you then.

It is too much for us. It is all too much for us. To have eaten what we have eaten. To have seen what we have seen. To know what we know. One day I prayed for hours and could only pray: "Yes. Yes. Yes, there is light. Yes, there is hope. Yes, there is love." Even though I felt none of it.

How do you sing a sacred song in a strange land? Maybe you just sing it. Maybe you don't attempt to be understood. Maybe you just sing what is so, because it is so. For the song's sake, for the singing's sake. Could I sing for the song's sake—for your sake, my sweet lamb of God? Could I sing you a lullaby as you lie cradled next to my heart shuddering in your mortality?

TONIGHT DIANA brought me a gift. "This is a prayer stick, Mom. I made it for you." It was a large stick with flowers woven round the top. Could I let the stick pray for me? For I do not know how to pray aright. I lean the stick against my altar. "Pray, stick," I say; "pray now." I go off to other things while the stick holds the offering pointing toward heaven. Dare I trust creation to pray for me, to bear my prayer? Here, stone, pray. Here, river, pray. Here, moon, pray. Just by being what you are, a maple branch salvaged from last fall's ice storm, wrapped round with pink petals, you are transformed by the touch of a child's hand into something sacred.

How shall we sing the Lord's song in a foreign land? That is the question. For our hearts are heavy and we, captive by this mortal flesh, sit down and weep.

Well, the Song Begins with *Yes* —
yes
body
like
a tube
a culvert
carrying
the earth's
refuse
twigs
garbage
whines
knotted, clotted, congealed evil, wads of anguish, passing through the yes into eternity cleansed and free. The yes like a filter, a rinse of spray. You can look at the sin or you can look at God. If you look too long at the evil, you will
become
frozen,
mesmerized
by it.
So head
on into
perfect
purity
and
funnel
the defiled
to
the undefiled
by virtue
of
your
yes.
Not my will but thine.

CHAPTER 16

Cranks, Crackpots, and Paul
Jesus and the Authentic Christ

While I was on my way and approaching Damascus, about noon a great light from heaven suddenly shone about me. I fell to the ground and heard a voice saying to me, "Saul, Saul, why are you persecuting me? . . . " Since I could not see because of the brightness of that light, those who were with me took my hand and led me to Damascus.

— ACTS 22:6-11

*J*went down to the ground, struck by a sickening blow to the gut. I went down to the ground, slamming against her unyielding firmness, the pitiless rock, as I yielded, as my flesh learned to release and part, to split and tear, to give. I went down to the ground. Sand pressed into my knees. Earth smeared into the rip of flesh. Stones entered me.

I went down until my face lay in the dust, until my body folded on itself in the dust, until my heart mingled with the dust, and I lay still in the dust, closed upon the ground like the wing of some great dead bird.

When I was lifted up from the ground, I was blind. Hands on my shoulders pulling me to my feet, hands dragging me away from the ground and her embrace, hands taking mine, took away my vision and day became night. I staggered and my sin was always before me.

You wonder if it happened, if I really saw what I say I saw, heard what I tell I heard. You wonder if I am mad or fabricating. See here, the proof is in my blindness, my stumble, my grope, and my stunned, numbed, nauseated soul walking like a refugee in a foreign land.

There are those who can testify that I saw well enough before, that I did not wear this unveiled shocked look of the newly blind. There are those who can remember the fervor and pulse of desire in me.

My mind shattered into brittle splinters, discrete thoughts, wholly separate, with no apparent connection to one another save my existence, the shabby stage on which they minced and raged. In darkness I paced that long night.

Then something like scales—some thing like scales, like slivers, husks, a tough membrane like scum—shucked from my eyes, and for the first time I saw the world like a worn pouch turned inside out.

When sight returned, there remained like a translucent cataract, Christ. Now between creation and me hangs that dear face. Upon it I gaze unceasingly and therein find All.

"It hurts you to kick against the goads," he said (Acts 26:14).

A BOOK CATALOG came the other day. I opened to a section called "Wisdom of the Ages" and read the entry for a new gospel according to Jesus. The author, seeking the most historically authentic depiction of Jesus, has retained only what the best of modern scholarship believes are the true words and acts of Jesus. The reader is assured that "the later accretions in which the evangelists had Church doctrine as their main purpose have been removed. Gone are the passages that try to prove that Jesus was the Son of God. Gone is the Jesus preaching hellfire and damnation in direct contradiction to the absolute forgiveness and unconditional love of the authentic Jesus."

Gone also, I might add, are any references to that troublesome accretion Paul. We have here a politically correct Jesus for our age, guaranteed to please all the folks and save none of them.

GOD BECKONS to us through the created order. We encounter and come to know Christ through persons, events, nature, and Scripture—the stuff of creation. We may mistake the creation for the Author of Creation, unwittingly endowing aspects of this earth with godlike character. But sooner or later we come to the limit of earthly existence and are knocked to the ground. We are broken into pieces. We learn that no matter how beautiful and mighty, the mountain is not God, the lover is not God, the song is not God. These only momentarily gave Eternal Love a shape and form for us to get to know it. God is forever beyond anything we can grasp or name. Then, as John of the Cross writes, we begin to discover creation in Christ: "And here lies the remarkable delight of this awakening: the soul knows creatures through God and not God through creatures."[16]

The figure/ground of our reality inverts. We no longer peer through creation seeking for a glimpse of God. Christ Jesus becomes the encompassing overarching actuality—rather than an illusive, sometimes present, sometimes absent possibility and promise in the context of a fallen created order. For now, creation itself is held within the sanctifying grace of the Savior.

> *"Saul, Saul, why are you persecuting me? It hurts you to kick against the goads."*

"Who are you, Lord?" I asked.

The Lord answered, "I am Jesus of Nazareth whom you are persecuting" (Acts 26:14–15).

THE CHRIST CHILD, whom we have been persecuting with our need to control and be right, reveals his divine origin, his sorrow, and his dwelling place in the heart of matter. Our false piety, self-righteousness, and sin are disclosed in the brightness of that light. Then we know we carry the most precious commodity in the universe in these earthen vessels.

After that, our relationship to ourselves, to God, and to creation is radically altered. We no longer bow to the cultural and religious norms but become bold to preach the gospel of Jesus Christ.

Quite a few people I know don't care much for Paul. But in these days, when tolerance seems to be valued over truth, I find comfort and encouragement in a fellow crank and crackpot. I am all for eccentricity and righteous indignation. This evolved as I began to notice that I had pretty well lost the race on most other counts. So a while back on the road to Holton, I resolved in a blast of light that I would hold out for eccentricity—the last frontier for the mature woman.

One could do a lot worse than look to Paul for guidance in that department. Yes, he is contentious, impetuous, even wrong from time to time. And so am I. Blinded by the light on that dusty road, he had given up all claims to himself and was discovered by a boundless freedom. It was as if something snapped in Paul. He was opened to a core of truth about which there could be no compromise. His loyalty was to Truth, to the One he had witnessed.

He gave up meeting any internal or external expectations other than the dazzling truth of Christ and him crucified. In that moment he became the authentic Paul. Minus any accretions, he became fully himself and human in the most unpretentious way, and hence truly holy. There was little about Paul personally that would win converts. He was no guru or cult leader. He would never be known as Rev. Feel-Good. He consistently pointed away from himself to Christ Jesus.

The difficult task for the disciples and part of the thrust of Paul's ministry was making the connection that the person of Jesus was the *Christ.* For some of today's disciples, the task is making a similar connection that the Christ is *Jesus.*

Jesus asks, "Who do you say that I am?" Peter and Martha respond, "I believe that you are the Christ." Today Christ addresses the modern world out of the mystery of galaxies, out of the suffering of the poor, out of an infant's eyes and asks, "Who do you say that I am?" Who is eccentric and bold enough to say, "I believe that you are Jesus"?

Without the historical enfleshing in Jesus and subsequent eternal presence in the Risen Lord, Christ is just a nice idea, a piece of metaphysics, a product of human need, a Gnostic doctrine. God heard our cry for Christ and incarnated in Emmanuel, thereby marrying time with eternity, the specific with the universal, the creation with the Creator. The name given to us for that action, which redeems and sanctifies each unique and individual expression of life, is Jeshua, Jesus. And it seems to me that it must surely please God for us to get the name right. We like to be known in our individuality, to be received and respected as ourselves, not as others would like to make us out to be.

Could this also be the desire of the Anointed One? Salvation stands at the door of creation and knocks, longing to be welcomed and known and loved for itself, its own distinct incarnate form, which found its fullest expression in the person of Jesus of Nazareth. Where is he? Where do we find the joy of our desiring? "Who do you say that I am?" he asks.

PART IV

. . .

A Refuge
and a Shelter

*Then the Lord will create over the whole site of Mount
Zion and over its places of assembly a cloud by day and
smoke and the shining of a flaming fire by night. Indeed
over all the glory there will be a canopy. It will serve as a
pavilion, a shade from the heat by day, and a refuge and
shelter from the storm and rain.*

— ISAIAH 4:5–6

The fundamental meaning of holy ground is safety. I am
amazed at how long it took me to understand that simple
and obvious truth. Only after repeated experiences of violated boundaries did I learn that it is no one's responsibility but my own to maintain and defend my sanctity.
Each of us is entrusted with a treasure and also with the
task of guarding that treasure.

My work turned out to be discovering what carried me to truth, hopping on and riding it into God's heart. I came to see that I am the ultimate authority on my reality. Further, I am accountable to God and to my brothers and sisters in creation for responsibly telling how I see things. The creation is waiting expectantly for each of us to express our unique vision. The full truth will not be known until we have fully told our individual truths. We must each run breathlessly out of the empty tomb of our lives and give faithful witness of our experience.

Much of my struggle had to do with the arduous process of discovering my truth and assuming my own spiritual authority. People frequently asked Jesus on what authority he forgave sins, healed, and preached with boldness. "Who do you think you are?" they asked. "What gives you the right?" Those are the very questions Turtle Street posed to me.

As I PARTICIPATED more and more in the mind of Christ, the locus of my internal authority shifted. God was realigning my will with God's will. My truth was becoming more like God's truth. Mortal flesh and blood resist such conforming. It hurt, just as my daughter's mouth hurt each time the orthodontist tightened her braces. My whole being ached, chafed, strained against the goads of Christ.

Although from the beginning I found support and encouragement from many generous people, I labored alone most of the time. Sometimes the sense of isolation was intense, and I searched for a church or praying community that had some understanding of this kind of ministry and that was willing to support me regularly with their prayers. Over time, I found community in many places.

For the most part Protestant mainline traditions do not have the structures to support prayer of this kind. The Roman Catholic and the Anglican traditions appreciate the need for a cloister, a place to support, nurture, and protect the contemplative. The Catholic and Orthodox Churches recognize the ministry of hermit or solitary as an important contribution to the work of the Church. My own forebears in the Society of Friends and the Amish Church had a healthy sense of the need for some kind of separation from the world. And my Jewish ancestors experienced the enforced cloister of the ghetto.

Occasionally I wonder what will happen as more and more persons, churched and unchurched, begin praying with greater depth and frequency. Will the Church at large know how to respond to and use the vital ministry of these individuals?

"IT IS IN DEEP SOLITUDE that I find the gentleness with which I can truly love my brothers," writes Thomas Merton.[17] The deeper and more sustained our prayer, the more sensitive and aware we become of the needs of the world. We also become better equipped to respond to the needs in redemptive ways. But oddly, this increased sensitivity may render some less able to be in the world for long periods without being debilitated by it.

Union with God seems to bring union with all that is in God, both the good and the evil. The same sensitivity that allows me, through prayer and laying on of hands, to bring relaxation and to hasten healing is what also brings on my fatigue, headaches, and illness when I neglect solitude. If I do not pray, if I do not seek solitude, I get sick. It's as simple as that. For one called to contemplation, solitude is not just a nice idea, a response of obedience, or a practice that will increase creativity and service; solitude is a requirement for health. Sustained prayer may leave us constitutionally unable to participate in a violent culture. Such prayer may eventually enforce lifestyle and cultural change, as a matter not only of conscience but of health.

1993–1995

CHAPTER 17

Telling the Truth
Setting Boundaries around Holy Ground

I picked up an issue of *Vanity Fair* while my daughters were getting their hair cut. On the cover was a photograph of Sharon Stone nude, her hands cupped over her breasts, with the caption: "Wild Thing! Sharon Stone's Other Instincts." Inside I read that Ms. Stone sees herself to be a manifestation of goddess energy.

On pages one and two was an ad for Ralph Lauren Safari, a cologne for men. It was a fuzzy photograph in nostalgic sepia tones of a man in a cowboy hat sitting behind the wheel of a jeep. He held a piece of grass in his teeth while gazing reflectively at a scene vaguely reminiscent of Africa. The large caption read: "Living without Boundaries."

Both Ms. Stone and Ralph made me nervous. And hearing my daughter tell the hairdresser, "Just a little off the ends, please. I'm growing out my bangs," I prayed: "Thank you, God, for boundaries."

"SET BOUNDS ABOUT THE MOUNTAIN," God commanded Moses. And apparently he did. When God commanded the prophet a second time to do the job, Moses, peeved, contested, "The people cannot come up to Sinai, for you yourself warned us saying, 'Set limits around the mountain and keep it holy.'"

There seems to be a double jeopardy here. The danger is both that the people would break through the boundaries in order to peek at God and thus perish from the sight of incinerating holiness, and that God would be defiled by proximity to mortal flesh and break out against those who trespass. The boundaries serve to protect God from the impurity of mortals and mortals from the purity of God.

Well, what did Moses do? How did he set those limits? Did he draw a line with chalk: "On this side you are safe and on the other is oblivion"? Did he pile up stones in a medicine circle around Sinai? Did he tack "No Trespassing" signs on trees? Did he steal out under the moon, mutter incantations, and sprinkle some fine invisible dust?

We know he told the people to clean up, do their laundry, get ready, and stay away from women. (By all means avoid that goddess energy and vanity's fair, bare throat and smooth shoulders.)

Once the fireworks got started—with the mountain belching flame and smoke, and the shophar blasting, and Sinai quaking, and thunder and lightning everywhere, and the priests busy sanctifying everything, and Moses dragging Aaron up the mountain—the people, scared witless, were more than happy to comply. Such obedience seemed to be the point of the whole affair, according to Moses and Calvin, namely, to instill a healthy dose of the fear of God, which seemed to be in short supply.

"You are a people holy to me," says the Lord. We come to know how holy we are by facing into the horror of how we have defiled and been defiled. The deepening awareness of the sins we have committed against one another is a function of the recognition of our call to holiness.

Yes, amazingly, we mortals participate in the holiness of God. And yet we somehow cannot be in the presence of one another without committing blasphemy, because we are at once a holy people and a sinful people. It is that paradoxical reality that demands bounds.

Holiness without bounds is vulnerability waiting to be abused. Boundaries are the means given to us, so that we can risk being together in community on this earth without violating one another's sanctity. To observe boundaries implies a willingness to be obedient, to surrender to powers wiser and greater than oneself.

So how does one set bounds? Sprinkle holy water around oneself? Hang garlic on one's door? Get a pet tarantula? Just tell the truth. Tell the truth. One must deeply claim and trust that one is holy and that God's word dwells and speaks within. When we doubt that, we waver and compromise our spiritual authority and succumb to the need to please and placate.

Jesus, who was truth, let the chips fall where they would. He called evil evil, hypocrisy hypocrisy, and sin sin. The truth, the bare truth that sets us free, sets the only boundary we need.

WE GOT A NEW DOG last spring. His name is Ahs, a name more properly exclaimed than pronounced. He is part collie and part sheep dog and finds his highest purpose and deep joy in herding. Most of his efforts are spent on Sarah, our thirteen-year-old hound who long ago learned to stay in line.

Nevertheless, Ahs cannot resist his breeding. He keeps constant vigilance, chewing Sarah's ears, nipping her back end, nudging and wrangling her. It's a shame we don't have a flock of sheep, some geese, and five or six more children ranging about the backyard for Ahs to corral. He is a natural Pharisee, keeping zealous tabs on order.

Moses could have used a dog like Ahs. Continually straying onto what we think are greener pastures, mindlessly munching and chewing, claiming there are no limits, showing up without our clothes on, bowing before golden calves, we all could use a good shepherd.

CHAPTER 18

Sitting Ducks
Freedom in Christ Jesus

*W*ho doesn't want to be effective, competent, and successful? Sometimes we may be tempted to apply the same criteria of achievement to our prayer as to material undertakings. Yet the journey of faith inspires in us a shift from finding our sense of competency in what we do and what we know to *whom we know and by whom we are known.* Christian spiritual growth encompasses the deepening reliance on our relationship with Jesus Christ for the center of meaning and purpose in our lives. Jesus, as the one in whom and through whom God has chosen to make divine reality known to the world, literally becomes the way, the truth, and the life. Through ongoing struggle and engagement with Jesus, we enter deep communion with our Source. A deepening relationship with Jesus is likely to uncover other competing sources of my sense of competency and meaning. In my discomfort and pain I discover what I am loving more than Jesus.

What the Christian offers of real power to transform and heal is not knowledge, skills, personal talents, and gifts, but rather the humble poverty of a relationship of loving intimacy with Jesus. This relationship informs and releases our service to creation. This is not to say that we ignore skill and knowledge altogether; but no knowledge or understanding we can ever attain can begin to compare with the healing and grace available to others through our relationship with Christ.

Such relationship renders us very vulnerable. I can control to some extent the know-how I shove into my brain and regurgitate out into the world. But when I stake everything on the risky, ever-changing nuances of a relationship with One beyond me, I surrender to faith. Few of us can stand to be so poor, so low. We may be terrified at the thought of being stripped of all that we use to prop ourselves upright. Our contempt for Jesus and our meager faith is exposed. We see our shame for Jesus in our nagging suspicion that he alone simply cannot be enough and in our fear of being so surrendered. Our doubt in the sufficiency of Christ may be exposed in our anxiety, despair, and compulsion to consume and acquire ever more knowledge.

This Jesus just leaves us so poor, so dependent—and so free. The freedom Jesus gives us is the freedom to be ourselves—our unadorned, weather-beaten, and world-weary selves.

For example, my husband and I had this old Toyota pickup. We kept it to haul things to the dump. For a while I drove it around town and out to the hermitage. It didn't have second gear, so it took a little finesse at slower speeds.

There was something about that pickup that stripped away my arrogance. One day when I bounced out to the hermitage to pray, I left behind the healthy "correct" retreat provisions: juices, bottled water, nuts and seeds in biodegradable bags. Instead, I tossed in a bag of Sterzing's potato chips.

These chips, made in Burlington, Iowa, are the chip of my childhood. In thirty some years, the red-and-white bag has remained the same. On the front is a cottage of the sort where Snow White might live and the words *Tri-Some!* cheerfully beckoning. Sterzing's prospers, fueled by the nostalgic memories of school lunch bags and family picnics. The chips, like us, have no redeeming qualities about them beyond being the best in God's good world.

When I got to the hermitage I pulled open the bag, breathed in the incense of its contents like a pleasing offering, and put my feet up on a prayer stool. Swilling a can of Pepsi and munching away, I hung out with Jesus. For some time I had thought that there might be a right way and a wrong way to pray, and I practiced several methods in the hope that I would get it right. But just hanging out, comfortable and satisfied, unadorned, weather-beaten, and world-weary, I was at the end of technique and the beginning of a relationship.

PAUL TOLD the Corinthians he wanted to know nothing but Christ and him crucified (1 Cor. 2:2). How could he stand to be so dumb? Remember Hans Christian Anderson's story "The Emperor's New Clothes"? The cunning thieves tell the emperor that only those who are fit for their office and not stupid will be able to see the fabulous clothes they fashion for the vain and foolish ruler. Of course emperor and subjects, not wanting to be declared unfit for their offices or stupid, fall for the scam and exclaim emphatically over the invisible garments. It is the little child who shouts the obvious truth that everyone has been assiduously denying: "The emperor is naked!"

Paul counts everything as loss because of the surpassing worth of knowing Christ Jesus. Sometimes it seems to me that few are desirous of knowing Christ Jesus and, further, that among those who are, a good many haven't the foggiest notion of how to make his acquaintance. Oh, we'd like Jesus to do nice things for us and for the world, but we'd prefer to know a lot of other things than the naked truth. I, for one, usually want to know what time it is or when we are going to get our bathroom remodeled.

Recently I read an article by a thirteen-year-old witch who knows a spell for protection. Now there is something worth knowing! The young pagan also advises the reader "to talk directly to the gods the same as Christians pray."

I wish I had a spell I could give to people. How about *Jesus Saves*, or *Let Go and Let God?* I see those on bumper stickers a lot. A while back, I saw *Keep on Praying*. I had about given up on praying till I saw that sticker. I confess, most days, I'd rather have a spell.

If I can open my heart and move through my hostility to Jesus, the long heritage of mortality obstinate to the divine, I might likewise begin to overcome my ego's natural aversion to my humanity—the self-condemnation, the urgent fretful drive for perfection, the never-satisfied scolding. I think there is a crucified savior in us all, crouching in the closets of our souls, suffering the jeers and disbelief.

Our resistance to Jesus—God choosing to become the most miserable of humans—is a reflection of our resistance to the sorry truth of ourselves, our inner shame and guilt. Just as we fail to receive God in divine vulnerability in the person of Jesus, we also fail to receive who we are in our sin and weakness.

Instead, we are scandalized by our imperfection. We are outraged and ashamed that we, wanting to be like God, are so full of frailty and fallibility. Growth in relationship with Christ requires letting go of the notion that we can be perfect, that around the bend, down the next aisle, at the end of this book, or in some psychological flim-flam, we will find that elusive wholeness we long for. Relationship with Jesus Christ begins with owning up to the fact that we are all vainly parading around like idiots in our birthday suits.

YOU NEVER KNOW what you are going to find on holy ground. I went out to the hermitage to pray one day. When I opened the sliding door off the porch, a dark animal much larger than a mouse scuttled along the wall. A quick survey around the room revealed feathers and droppings. Crouched in the alcove next to the bed facing the wall sat a small black duck. How she found her way into the locked hermitage is a mystery.

That evening a friend told me a Lakota Sioux story of Iktomi and the ducks. I went to bed and dreamed of ducks.

> Iktomi, the spider woman, wanted some ducks to eat. So she told the gullible creatures that she would teach them how to dance a sacred dance. "A sacred dance!" the ducks exclaimed. "Let us learn to do a sacred dance. Oh, how wonderful! Think how beautiful we will look, how graceful we will be, how special we will become. Once we know such a splendid thing as a sacred dance, we will have power, freedom, fame, and all the frogs we can eat."
>
> Iktomi assured the ducks that all their dreams and more would come to pass if they would learn the dance.
>
> "Teach us this dance," the ducks begged eagerly.
>
> "I will teach you what no other duck has ever known, but first you must come into my tent, for this is esoteric knowledge hidden from the common world." And she ushered the ducks into her tent, where they sat solemnly with barely contained zeal.
>
> "Before you can learn the sacred dance," she began, "you must of course know the holy song."
>
> The ducks were crestfallen. "The holy song! But we don't know the holy song," they cried in alarm.
>
> "No problem," Iktomi counseled. "I will teach you. But first you must gather closer to me so I do not have to strain my voice. And you must close your eyes in order to clear your mind to receive this divine mystery."
>
> The ducks waddled closer in a tight ring around Iktomi. Each taking various pious postures that they'd seen in pictures of saints, they beatifically closed their eyes, cleared their throats and opened their beaks in preparation for the song. In a flash Iktomi grabbed a duck by its neck and thrust it in her sack. But just as she was reaching for another, one duck opened its eyes and, squawking, sounded the alarm. Honking freedom, they spread their wings, and the sitting ducks danced right out of Iktomi's tent and flew over the lake in a sacred getaway.

All that glitters is not gold. The emperor has no clothes. You cannot know a sacred dance in the same way you can know the capital of South

Dakota. For Truth, who keeps asking, "Who do you say that I am?" is not something one knows but rather a relationship in which one *is known*.

Once, inspired by Paul, I prayed to know nothing but Christ and him crucified. I don't recommend it. Everything else went out of my head. I babbled like an idiot, and a cross loomed over me off to the right with a massive Jesus leaning over the world. I was filled with a strange and terrible kind of joy. As I beheld the dying God, all I felt was love pouring from the cross like streams of thick cream.

I wanted to go up to strangers in the supermarket, shout, and point at Christ hanging over the frozen pizza, "Look at that! Look at that! Redemption doesn't come cheap!"

I KNELT DOWN by the duck in the hermitage. As I reached my palm toward her I thought how very strange my hands would feel upon her back. Never before to have known the press of human flesh upon her wings, how frightening to be grasped by slim, naked, jointed sticks, to be lifted by a power other than her own. Would she be able to surrender to such confinement in order to receive freedom? Would my touch of salvation be gentle and safe enough to not send her into panic?

> O Holy One,
> make my touch like prairie wind,
> like quiet ripples of pond water,
> like mossy green algae alive with plankton,
> like swaying grass on the shore.
> Make my entry into her captivity
> known and familiar as one of her own kind,
>   a sister duck.

She remained calm as I lay my palms over her. Lifting her quickly, I walked outside and released my grasp. Her wings unfolded in a whoosh, as she soared out over the water in the morning sun.

CHAPTER 19

A Holy Song
Discernment and the Will of God

*S*ix-year-old Diana, resplendent in my old prom dress, yards of purple-and-green chiffon trailing behind her and four necklaces hanging to her waist, chatters and chirps as she digs in my desk drawers. She hauls out the magnifying glass from the Oxford English Dictionary and inspects my back for bugs. She pulls down all the small "just my size" prayer books and brandishes the *Scottish Book of Common Prayer*. Sweeping ceremoniously over to the Indian bells hanging on a rope, she solemnly announces, "Now I will sing a holy song!" Accompanying herself on bells, she chants in a wavering pitch: "What do you waant? Oh please tell us what you waant."

Well, that does seem to be the question, doesn't it? Century after century we keep getting all dressed up. Toting books of incantations and rituals, we chant in our best devotional tones: What do you want? Oh please tell us what you want.

We really would like to get it right. There is in us a passion to please, a longing to lay ourselves down in acceptable service before the great powers of the universe. And beneath the longing for our gifts to be received may be the vague and disturbing notion that not being received may mean sure disaster.

How can you tell what God wants? How can you distinguish a bad spirit from a good spirit when Satan is reputed to appear as an angel of light? How do you sort through the multiple inner voices to determine which carry truth, which whisper sedition, which lead into temptation, and which open you to greater freedom and intimacy with God? How do you sift the fine sands of emotional states, temperaments, and personal history? What are your blind spots and addictions? Which is a true attraction of the heart and which is heartburn? Where does desolation end and PMS begin?

Cain got it wrong. What he offered God and had every reason to believe God wanted was not accepted. One thing led to another. Cain's countenance fell. Sin burst through the door. Cain rose up and killed his brother. What was wrong with Cain's offering? Why did God not accept the sacrifice at his hands? In contradiction to the claims of Calvin and other interpreters, there is nothing to disqualify Cain. He came before God offering his best. Scripture gives no reason for the rejection.

Old Testament scholar Walter Brueggemann chalks God's inexplicable behavior up to "the capricious freedom of Yahweh."[18] Yahweh's "jerkness," I'd say. Too much theology tries to protect God's hind parts. Too much of what passes for virtue is an apology for a God who does not need placating, obsequious protection, as much as defiant confrontation by a creature who knows its own dignity.

WHEN I ASKED Diana to sing her holy song again for me, she hesitated. "You won't laugh?" she asked.

After Cain had run away to Nod, maybe God felt really sorry. Maybe the whole rest of salvation history is God making it up to Cain. Maybe not. "Life is unfair. God is free," writes Brueggemann.[19] And because this is true, asking what God wants is a harrowing question that exposes our souls to shame and danger. And that is why I told Diana I would not laugh.

There are numerous approaches to discerning God's will. What the methods have in common is a thoughtful, prayerful sifting of what is being given—the facts, the feelings, the circumstances, the desires—conducted in an atmosphere of honesty and acceptance. These are held up against Scripture, tradition, and the community of faith. What follows is a more or less mad leap into the unknown. Beyond what seems at times the minimally satisfactory promise that God will be with us, there are no guarantees.

It is excruciating when our discernment proves false, when God has no regard for our gifts, when our best is not enough. At such moments we can appreciate Cain's rage and the temptation to murder one's rival. "How can he be so accepted? How could I have been so wrong? I prayed. I asked for guidance. I listened. I waited for confirmation. I had faith—what went wrong?"

WE FEEL SEDUCED, led astray, and abandoned by a deceitful God. We feel ashamed, bitter, and mistrusting. Our ability to offer ourselves freely in love again and to receive love from this One who has hurt us so may become crippled.

In any encounter with God, we would do well to remember that we might be dealing with a maniac. Given the catastrophic weight of anguish and injustice in creation, you'd have to be a dimwit not to have such a thought from time to time.

Through the hellish experience of rejection and loss, we become sadder but wiser. A theology of protest and suspicion quietly emerges founded, not on the fact of evil and human sin but on our conviction of the holiness that resides in mortals. This faith grows out of our deepening appreciation for the immaculate tenderness, the inner holy ground that supports all things. We begin to identify this goodness with the indwelling Christ.

The issue in discernment is not so much making the right decision as allowing all our life choices, right and wrong, to lead us to our true voice, our authentic self where Christ dwells. The task is to obey the voice we think is true with all the devotion we can muster, even if ultimately the voice proves false, because that is the only way we make the arduous journey to the deepest truth within us.

As we reflect on our choices over time, we learn to discriminate with greater precision among the many competing voices. We come to recognize the shepherd's voice and to identify that voice with our truest self. We begin to make the bold and awesome connection that my *I* and Christ's *I* are one, just as he promised. I have found my voice and God's voice has found me. And we are one.

To have a voice is to have the right of speech, influential power, a distinctive form of expression that is genuinely oneself. To have voice is to possess authority. Now we become bold to challenge God. Instead of taking up the unfairness of God's activity in our lives with our brother or sister by killing him or her, we take it up with God. In order to do that with integrity and power one needs a sense of one's self as a creature worthy of doing business with the Lord God.

"Intercession is spiritual defiance of what is, in the name of what God has promised," writes Walter Wink.[20] The Bible demonstrates that God can make a mistake. We find the long history of biblical protest in which complaints and charges are brought against God. Abraham argues for Sodom. Moses defends the stiff-necked people. Jeremiah calls God a deceitful brook. Job and the psalmists hold God accountable to being God. Many have taken it upon themselves to point out to God occasions of divine ungodliness.

Such a prayer of protest proclaims faith as powerfully as the prayer of surrender. For strangely, we know the promise of God for wholeness and peace is real in its negation. Our very suffering testifies that things ought not to be this way. The flesh protests. The heart protests. The mind protests. Even if we feel unable to protest—even if we feel too confused, too trapped, and too hopeless to ever extricate ourselves from bondage, the testimony to God continues in our depression, in our lack of vitality, and in our physical ailments. For if God's promises to us were not real and our rightful inheritance, it would never occur to us to protest.

The stance toward God of wise suspicion and defiant protest is not a bullying show of bravado. It is not an attitude put on at an assertiveness-training seminar. It is not a function of a power suit, the right credentials, or an imposing physique. What is it that wins us peership with God in such matters? What gives us the right?

In Matthew a woman gets lippy with Jesus. Insistent in the face of rejection, this Canaanite shockingly engages with Jesus as a peer. "Get her out of here. Her shouting bothers us. Has she no shame?" the crowd wonders. Well, the fact is she has no shame—and therein rest her authority and faith.

She does not grovel or beg. She does not flatter or seduce. She respectfully, if not quietly, demands healing for her daughter and is not deterred from her purpose. When Jesus tells her that healing Canaanites is not part of his job description, she holds him accountable and at this point seems to know more about his mission than he does. She challenges and expands Jesus' "self-definition," just as the crisis of suffering and injustice her daughter endures likely has reformed the woman's understanding of who she is.

The fruit of hardship, illness, and calamity is shame. Disaster exposes our vulnerability to the harsh scrutiny of the world. When the protective cloak of personal dignity is ripped away, we lose touch with our innocence and right to blessing as God's holy children. This is not to excuse our sin and evil, but the final word from God to us is redemption not condemnation, acceptance not blame. And it is that Word made flesh for us and in us in Jesus Christ on which we base our defiance.

Christ sets us free from the paralysis of shame. Christ's small voice becoming more and more our own voice grants us full stature as God's holy people. In Christ we recover our innocence and become no less than the righteousness of God.

The Canaanite woman courageously moves toward an oppressive and threatening culture and religious system. Jesus ignores her. The disciples complain. She balances between a faith in the innocence and righteousness of her child and a faith in Jesus as the one who has the capacity and responsibility to heal. Her daughter is healed as a consequence of an exchange between a mortal and the Son of God in which both parties are in full possession of their authority.

Healing requires justice and justice requires courage.[21]

CHAPTER 20

The Dying Pear Tree
Desire and Detachment

Eternity, my child, is a golden cord tied to the throat of God. Eternity's cord tethers God to us. Look, there, out in the backyard, God grazing under the pear tree! Take a sugar cube. Walk up softly. No sudden movements. Feel the soft lip of God on your palm. See his teeth.

*T*he pear tree is dying. The county extension agent came and looked it over. "There is nothing you can do," she said breaking off a slab of bark. "Pear trees don't live long."

There is a narrow gash in its trunk. Last summer the kids stuck things in the opening—twigs, flowers, tiny rocks, like offerings. Death extends along the north side of the tree like a poisonous vine. Today in the late winter sun I cannot tell which branches are alive and which are dead.

The pear was splendid last fall. Flaming pink, russet, and orange, the dying tree recklessly spent itself in beauty. It gave glory to the days without discrimination. Brilliant blue heaven or still gray sky, it blazed the same.

Passion draped upon a tree. Love cracked opened and poured out upon our hearts, spreading like a bright stain. Who or what can stay this bleeding heart of love? Who can bear its sweetness? Who is pure enough to touch its petals? Is there one whose ferocity will guard the sacred precincts? One whose strong arm wields the sword with swift, sure certain aim?

SOME SAY DESIRE is the cause of all suffering. To escape suffering, one needs to stop desiring and become detached. I don't think so.

Several years ago, when we said good-bye to family and friends after a wedding to make the long drive home, Diana sobbed in the back seat. She

90

didn't want to leave the festivities—the flowers and the cake, the beautiful bride and groom, the music and the dancing guests. She wept for miles, keeping track of the number of tissues she used. "Twenty-nine," she sobbed. "Thirty," snuff. "Thirty-one," sniffle. "My heart is broken. I will never be happy again," she mourned. Finally, exhausted, she fell asleep around tissue sixty-two.

Things matter. Things matter a lot. We hunger and thirst. We desire and need. We lust after and long for. The bolder ones among us ride the current of their passion into the world like fearless surfers.

I have a friend who has laid down his life for the poor and homeless. Today he lies in a room without enough money to buy the fortified drink he needs to stay alive. He is dying of the same disease as those he served.

This friend gave me a picture of Jesus with eyes that followed me about the room. In the center of Christ's chest was a red heart surrounded with thorns. Flames rose from the wounded heart and light radiated all around it. On the back my friend wrote, "May the searching and compassionate eyes of Christ and the burning love of his heart always be with you."

Yes, I will follow you. Yes, I will lay my body down. Yes, they say, and dash like fools across the street never looking both ways.

The immutable laws of nature hold. The earthquake is unmoved by cries for mercy. The bullet neatly severs the spine. The flesh is fragile, frail, and shy. And we do not do the good we want, but the evil we do not want is what we do.

Write a note to a pear tree in tiny script. Slip it into the wound at the new moon. "Don't die. Please don't die." Still, trees age and die. And saviors slump against the cross.

TO DESIRE, to reach toward something or someone beyond oneself, is a gift from God. Desire motivates us into the world. It keeps us growing and learning and creating. Desire is part of what it means for us to be in God's image, for desire is an important aspect of God's own nature. The jealous God of Israel, fuming and weeping, pleading and dying, is hardly detached.

Our desire is often conflicted, enmeshed, entangled, and confused. We are not sure what we want a good deal of the time. And when we are sure, we are ashamed and embarrassed to state our needs. We are fearful of needing much of anything very badly. We deceive ourselves about what we really want and chase after things that cannot truly satisfy.

The passion of our youth may be so battered by the inevitable betrayals of human existence that all that remains is a dry husk, an empty pod, the fuel of ardor long since spent. Housed in brittle skepticism, we become tentative, defensive, and guarded against the madness of love. Having been more sorry than we ever could have anticipated, we decide it is better to be safe.

Sometimes what passes as spiritual detachment, the letting go that heralds deepening trust in God, is really dissociation, the unconscious defense that blesses a soul in trauma. The movement to detachment and the place beyond pleasure and pain ought never to be at the expense of the full and hearty expression of the suffering. When pain becomes intolerable, the flesh and the heart grow numb. Nothing matters. Everything is the same. Passion is dead. Injustice is accepted without protest. What is redeeming about Christ's death is not that he transcended the pain, but that he felt it all the way. So I say: holler and wail and use up all the tissues you need!

Passion requires education and purification. It needs limits to protect it. In the beginning passion does not protect itself. It trusts the beloved to protect it. Through reversals, losses, and its own crucifixion, passion comes to respect itself enough to exercise discrimination. Then passion is defended by truth, by the free expression of the authentic self. What has to happen for it to be safe enough for you to let her rip? Just the courage to tell the truth and a fierce reverence for your own holiness.

Passion is premised on an object. Desire requires a beloved. Longing feeds on separation. At-one-ment is our reparation. Atonement both protects and satisfies passion. Before atonement—or the union with God made available to us through the fully expressed suffering of Christ—my passion is reckless, addicted, and self-destructive. There is something out there I need in order to feel whole and complete. Passion wants to possess, to take the beloved for itself. When we follow Jesus to the cross, God educates our passion to find its fulfillment in appreciation and gratitude rather than ownership. Through union with God won by the passion of God's beloved, our passion is surrendered for divine purposes as we become one with what we have loved. Then living or dying, like the pear tree, we blaze the same.

CHAPTER 21

At the Threshing Floor
Lemonade, Suffering, and the Abundant Life

*T*he kids were busy setting up a lemonade stand, and I braced myself for the sticky kitchen floor and a trail of ants under the door. They hauled out the card table, set it up in the shade under the maple, and made signs. The alarming discovery that we were out of lemonade and cups sent us to the grocery store. After deliberating for several minutes over the best cups to buy, my daughters spontaneously embraced me in the paper products aisle telling me they loved me, pushing each other away to give me kisses.

As we headed out, Cicelia said, "Mom, I just get this funny feeling in my tummy when you buy things for us."

"It's guilt," observed her older sister sagely. "Mom, you are just too nice sometimes. And it makes us feel bad."

Once someone wrote to me asking help for what she referred to as her gift/curse of feeling so deeply the pain of her suffering friend that she frequently became incapacitated. More recently, another person dedicated to intercessory prayer told his painful struggle with being faithful to this call. Someone else confessed she was a bit confused about the difference between "redemptive suffering and suffering suffering."

I recall a seminary classmate raising her hand and saying that when she prayed for others she felt their pain. "Is there any way to avoid that?" she asked. The professor was silent for a long moment, then responded simply, solemnly, "No."

WHAT IS THE MYSTERIOUS and perplexing relationship between suffering and redemption? Why do we have to hurt in order to get well? Why must the healer suffer along with the one who seeks health? Why is abundance so hard to receive without feeling guilty?

Looking for some answers, I read a new book on prayer. The book, by a physician, explores whether prayer is as valid and vital a healing tool as are drugs and surgery. The author presents scientific research attesting to prayer's efficacy. I already knew that prayer heals. I read the book hoping I could learn how to pray without getting sick myself, but the author didn't address this aspect. His approach was largely utilitarian—how to most effectively use this mysterious power for others' welfare, what techniques seem to work best, and so on. Nothing wrong with that, I suppose. But what I found missing was a lack of concern for being in relationship with this power.

I find a similar lack of concern for relationship in our culture's cheerful worship of the power of mind over matter and in our present infatuation with spiritual experience and the technology of consciousness. Of such activities, Evelyn Underhill wrote:

> In every period of true mystical activity we find an outbreak of occultism, illuminism, or other perverted spirituality and—even more dangerous and confusing for the student—a border-land region where the mystical and psychical meet.[22]

We can learn to use our minds to lower our blood pressure and sometimes to heal ourselves from cancer, but ultimately neither the universe nor God is subject to our will and control. Therefore it is important to discern the differences among the primitive magical thinking of a child who assumes his or her thoughts cause events, the development of our mental powers for ours and others' well-being, and prayer.

We ought not to confuse such practices as some forms of meditation and the development of the mind for personal well-being and healing with the practice of prayer. In one case I train the power of my consciousness to reduce stress and promote health. In the other, I surrender my power and ask for healing for others and myself simply by virtue of my loving relationship with God.

One approach says, "I will heal you or myself. It is self-conscious, controlled, examined, and studied for its effectiveness." The other approach says, "I will ask Jesus Christ to heal you." It is self-forgetting and surrendered. Through such intercessory prayer, help comes into the world not because I possess some skill or virtue but simply because I have been given the unmerited gift of knowing Christ Jesus.

WHAT IS RIGHT relationship for me with God, with self, with creation? What pleases God? What offends God? What is required of me for intimacy with the Trinity? How do I come to know Jesus? And is it possible to pray for others without suffering myself?

According to contemporary research on moral development, these are just the sort of questions a woman might ask. Kathleen Fischer writes:

> Gilligan's research on moral development indicates that men are generally more concerned with autonomy and achievement, while women give priority to relationships of interdependence . . . Whereas models of human development drawn largely from male experience indicate that a person matures through separation, autonomy, and individualization, women's experience suggests that a woman's sense of self is organized around being able to make, then to maintain affiliation and relationships. This means that at the core of her person is interest in and attention to the other person and expectation of a relationship as a process of mutual sensitivity.[23]

This feminine emphasis on relationship lies near the heart of the biblical understanding of redemption. For the root meaning of redemption carries the notion of relationship. When Ruth crawled in stealth across the threshing floor to rouse the groggy Boaz guarding his grain and boldly appealed to him, "Throw your cloak over me for you are my *goel*," a foreign woman was calling an Israelite man to responsibility (Ruth 3). By this undertaking she cooperated with the providential movement of grace into the world and became a bearer of the promise of salvation.

Goel, the Hebrew word frequently translated as "redeemer," means literally the next of kin who marries a widow, thereby saving her from a life of destitution. A *goel* delivers a relative from captivity or loss. In the Book of Job, *goel* is equivalent to protector, vindicator, savior. *Savior* is a word that stands for several Greek and Hebrew words, the general idea being one who brings safety, health, soundness, and freedom from the dominion and curse of sin.

The Book of Ruth is a protest against narrow nationalism and a plea for the inclusion of foreigners in the assembly of Israel. It is a tale of the trust and affection between women who move forward the purposes of God through innovative radical action. In her journey from destitution to wholeness and well-being, Ruth conceives and delivers salvation. Because of Ruth's radical action (encouraged by another relative, her mother-in-law, Naomi), she is numbered among the foremothers of Jesus Christ. The child born to her and Boaz is the grandfather of King David.[24]

When Ruth tells Boaz, "You are my goel," she calls him to account by insisting that he rise to the full stature of his responsibility in his relationship with her. She says, "Be who you are: be compassionate, be responsible, be powerful, be saving." Redemption is accomplished as the one in power responds out of his or her privilege and invites the weaker family member under the protective cover of that privilege.

AN INTERCESSOR is one who joins with Christ to stand in the treacherous gap between heaven and earth. As in the original Hebrew meaning of the word "priest," the healer or intercessor stands before God on behalf of the people. Redemption comes not by any particular skill or technique but simply by virtue of the relationship of the intercessor with God and with the one prayed for. This standing between—and it does require *standing* in the sense of strength and holding one's ground—involves a mutual calling to account: holding God accountable to being God, to being merciful and mighty, and holding the creation accountable to being holy children of God and redeemers with Christ.

Hence relationship is not only a key element in women's development but also in our understanding of redemption. And this is also where the waters become muddy. Fischer continues:

> Because relationship is so important to her, a key spiritual issue for a woman is how to live out the demands of Christian love. She struggles to balance care of others with care for self. . . . Agape or self sacrificial love has been offered to women as the highest ideal, thus reinforcing the socialization process that has already schooled a woman to place another's needs before her own.[25]

To care for one's self, to advocate and intercede for one's self, feels selfish to some. If I meet my needs, won't someone else suffer? Am I not supposed to deny myself? We may stand like Diana and Cicelia, immersed in guilt with our grocery cart filled with just what we wanted.

IN MY EXPERIENCE, this dilemma does not belong to women alone. Male or female, the more we pray, the more sensitive we become. The deeper our union with Christ, the deeper our union with all that is in Christ. Our global village exposes us to the suffering of others with anguished immediacy and intimacy. As we participate in the consciousness of Christ, we become acutely aware of our personal suffering, of the suffering of others, and of our privilege.

There is a destitute widow and a Boaz snoozing on his full belly in each of us. Need and privilege. Weakness and power. Masculine and feminine. At the urging of wise old Naomi, the Ruth in us is invited to defy custom, make her own decisions, and work salvation by awakening the inner wealthy Boaz and holding it accountable for her protection—because in order for action to be redemptive, it must flow from the marriage of strength and vulnerability.

The threshing floor is the holy ground where what is essentially feminine comes before what is essentially masculine. Here is where I meet the redeemer. Here is where I speak for myself, where I am recognized for what I am—loyal and heroic. (Boaz calls Ruth a worthy woman.) And here is where I receive abundance.

What happens when you seek to hold privileged individuals accountable to responding to your or creation's poverty and suffering? They may declare in a rush of resentment and bitterness that they are the ones in need, that they are the ones wronged. It is as though Boaz sits up and says, "Wait a minute, Ruth. You have no idea what I have been through. The crops are bad this year. I have suffered this and that. I have no resources left. I am as much a widow as you. I have all I can do to take care of myself."

If I am a Boaz who is estranged from my Ruth, my own deep need, I will feel contempt and impatience with myself and others. I will feel threatened by their needs, and I will hoard my harvest. If I am a Ruth who is estranged from my Boaz, my own power and abundance, I will see and feel the needs of the world, but my compassionate action will soon leave me drained, hopeless, and destitute.

It is the Ruth in us hesitating at the threshing floor who wonders if it is possible to enjoy abundant life while her sisters and brothers suffer. Yet it will be because of Ruth's action that Naomi's future is secured and the lineage of Jesus established.

And it is Boaz in us, turning over in the chill to behold the beautiful Ruth silhouetted in the moon, who exclaims, "Well what have we here? This is one fantastic woman! I believe there is more than enough to go around."

So Ruth tiptoes home at dawn with her veil filled with six measures of barley and a husband up her sleeve.

Since God chose to redeem us by taking on our illness, I suppose we ought not to expect that, in our efforts to be healers, we might escape tasting the suffering of others. The purpose of God's people, the covenant community, is exemplified by Isaiah's suffering servant:

> By his wounds we are healed/. . . through him the will of the LORD shall prosper./Out of his anguish he shall see light/. . . because he poured out his soul to death/and was numbered among the transgressors; yet he bore the sin of many/and made intercession for the transgressors. (53:5, 10, 12)

For such suffering to be redemptive, we are required to be in possession of our own wealth and privilege, that is to say, aware of our strengths and gifts. We need to name and claim our personal power without shame or apology. Then we need to apply the prosperity of Boaz with compassionate generosity to ourselves.

IN THIS TIME of great affluence, a good many persons live in a chronic state of emotional and spiritual deprivation or widowhood. They can never do enough, be enough, own enough. They suffer from an addiction to perfection, a cruel litany of personal put-downs, of harsh shoulds and oughts, an oppressive burden of brutality toward themselves that surely causes the angels to shrink in horror.

Could we see ourselves clothed in abundance, resting in luxury, welcoming our poor needy selves with the reverence and eager hospitality reserved for an honored guest? For the widow has much to offer the man of wealth—something that his money cannot buy. Aging Boaz, delighted that Ruth has come to him and not to a younger man, is no fool. He knows this alliance will be of mutual benefit.

The sin of many is not selfishness but the denial of the true self. We fail to uncover and respond to the most vulnerable part of ourselves—the core of our being where Christ dwells—and to believe its truth, to have compassion for its reality and, thereby, to redeem it and be made whole by its sacrifice and suffering.

We love, we pray, we intercede, we redeem with Christ, only because we have first been loved. If we cannot receive God's grace-filled love into our hearts, our efforts as healers will surely destroy us. If we do not know and taste that sweet flowing abundance, it may be time to wake up Boaz and have a glass of lemonade.

PART V

• • •

That Our Joy May Be Complete

One of Diana's first words was "bye." She was less than a year old, and I was still saying hello to her.

Change and movement are intrinsic to creation. Completion is illusory. Turtle Street is a series of countless deaths, a long succession of good-byes and letting go. For a while I tried to build booths and monuments to enshrine and preserve what I loved the way I loved it. I can only nod and acknowledge my beloved on the wing, waving as it passes by on its way to fulfilling its destiny. I cannot possess, but I can appreciate. And this, in the end, may be all God wants from us—to be appreciated—to be noticed, greeted, looked at, and listened to with attentiveness and gratitude. Isn't this pretty much what we all want? Isn't this love?

In a long struggle to obtain something I wanted very much from God, I learned to let go. Just when I had let go as much as I thought I possibly could, God would ask me to let go even more. Over and over I fell into the miry swamp of my unfaith, where I flailed about, running from the alligators snapping at my heels.

This life of prayer required sacrifices of my family and me. We lived a good deal of the time on one income. I struggled with feelings of inadequacy as I forfeited pension, insurance, and the esteem I sometimes imagined I would feel in a parish job. I fretted that few colleagues and fewer lay persons understood or appreciated this ministry. Without the day-to-day human contact and structure of an institution, I sometimes felt isolated. I wanted to offer my daughters more financially. I worried that remaining in a small rural town might leave them educationally and culturally deprived. When I turned fifty and recalled that I had been voted most likely to succeed by members of my high school graduating class, I was distressed that I did not possess some of the signs of success some of my peers had. I felt ashamed to have no more than a borrowed one-room cabin in a pasture to show for my two master's degrees.

Then one day, instead of praying for my cherished desire or for God's will to be done (this varied with the fluctuations of my faith), I was inspired to ask for a heart of gratitude and joy. I had never had a prayer so instantly answered in the positive. I was handed not what I had longed for but something better: all that I had imagined I would feel and become in possessing what I desired.

Of course the gratitude and joy weren't permanent. Like most of God's consolations, they preserved me until God saw I was ready for more letting go. Then I slammed into some new evidence of my attachment to the world. God held me while I argued, whined, and pouted until, at last, weary of kicking and stomping my feet, I surrendered my willfulness to the mystery of God's providential love. Then there was a bit more uncluttered room in me for God to dwell. Self-emptying and purgation, the saints called it. A loathsome practice by any name.

1995-1996

CHAPTER 22

My Sister Is Praying Today
Famished for the Truth

A contemplative is not someone who takes his prayer seriously,
but someone who takes God seriously, who is famished for the truth.
—THOMAS MERTON

My sister is praying today. My sister is praying in the forest. She is sitting in the forest praying, turning us like pebbles in her palms, feeling our edges between her thumb and forefinger, rubbing us like beads back and forth, over and over, counting our scars, telling our wounds, singing our hope, clicking us together in her palms as the ticking planet turns.

We come and go, riding down freeways, standing in checkout lines, wheeling into operating rooms, folding laundry, driving tractors across the crumbling earth.

Can you hear her prayer? Sometimes it is a soft hum, a buzz, or the whirring plop of closing ventricles. Does her passion penetrate your pain? Can you hear the sobbing of the souls she rocks?

As she stood at the window watching the trees, waiting for a sign, something gave in my sister's belly, a soft releasing, and she sank to her knees.

Always I have lain against this cheek, yet never known till now.
Always my hungry heart did seek to know this palm upon my brow.

Always I have ached to touch your face; always this urgent press upon my thigh.
Always I have been in this embrace, this vision pure before my eye.

Always I have sought you seeking me, whose eager reaching I had fled;
Till thirst for any touch but thine alone was from me bled.

When I was all a mortal wound, bleeding hope, thought, affection, will,
Then I fell through the jagged hole in space our bodies fill.

And there you gently wrapped me with your substance round;
  There covered my nakedness with yours.
There we dance emptiness from form unbound.
  There from our empty hearts form pours.

When this prayer was finished, she watched a spider fashion a web in the space where the ceiling met the wall. The spider worked quickly weaving a trap in the cleft where two directions collided to catch her supper.

My sister's second prayer was longer. It lasted days, weeks, who knows? The moon grew and shrunk, grew and shrunk. She babbled, lost her bearings, wandered in her found edges, and roamed over the cosmos into foreign galaxies.

Maybe this time you felt her prayer—a misty wisp of memory like a cashmere shawl descending on you as you were reading the paper, a shift in the wind, a change in conditions, an altering of plans, a break, an opening, a flood of tears, perhaps a sudden somewhat subtle slit in what had been the seamless garment of your suffering.

My sister's prayer:

> *Laid open again! Falling down a tunnel, tumbling over and over, fumbling for the cure. Have mercy! I cannot learn this dance. I hurt, caught in the crack between two worlds. I have not yet got the knack of walking through walls. This time I did not get out in time.*
>
> *What am I to do with this love? Teach me the password to unlatch the hidden gate in the substance that holds things hoped for. O Jesus, save us! Is this where you were for those three days?*
>
> *O Rose. O Fire. Sore rife! How many trips dare you make cradling form to your heart? How many times can you wrest them out of the flame and carry them over in your teeth to drop them before the other flame? How many times can you dive into the lake before the lake sucks you in and clamps on you her claim?*

This praying was getting to her and, for a while, my sister thought of her hunger—of juicy oranges, of thick potato soup, of the solid comfort of one against whom she could lean and discover herself in her own resistance to the press of flesh.

She walked down the path searching for a place to lay our grief, a cave to cover our nakedness. She looked into the stream to see if she was there. A brown leaf in flames spun in circles and floated south. She placed her foot upon the water. Would it hold her weight? She longed to fling herself against one or the other—to step into space and fall free or to cozy up next to the shape of things to come and say at last, "This is this and that is that." She yearned to see truth pinned, wings spread across a wall and underneath on a small white card to have read: Here, this is it. This is All.

MY SISTER PRAYS while we wait for righteousness. Under the moon she mixes potions, a balm for all wounds. She tends her daughter, Ambiguity, nursing her at her breast, brushing her hair. "Who are you child?" she asks. "Where have you come from?"

"I come from the threshold. Hold me to the light, I change. Dip me in water, I disappear. Taste me, and I will eat your heart out."

My sister is praying today. My sister is praying in the forest. She is sitting in the forest praying, turning us like pebbles in her palms, feeling our edges between her thumb and forefinger, rubbing us like beads back and forth, over and over, counting our scars, telling our wounds, singing our hope, clicking us together in her palms as the ticking planet turns.

Have you heard her prayer? Did you know she is there, walking barefoot where few other dare, slowly, painfully igniting herself for our sakes into one immaculate, incandescent, and solitary flare?

PRAYER CHANGES THINGS. What changes most is likely to be the one praying, as my sister is painfully discovering. Transformation summons us to new uncharted regions of being. Sometimes sad Golgotha feels safer than that empty tomb yawning hope. "Happiness is never so welcome as changelessness," wrote Graham Green.[26] We may pause on the threshold of change, shrinking in despair. What can I do? Every way I know to respond is unsatisfactory. I have tried this; I have tried that. My resources are bankrupted. I have come to the end of my known world.

At the place of impasse we are likely to try to do what we have done before, now with increased determination, only to suffer repeated defeat and betrayal. It takes considerable strength and equanimity to stand the ambiguity and tolerate the tension of the lack of resolution characteristic of impasse.

We are stubbornly loyal to our crosses. Is it possible to embrace abundance without denying crucifixion? Can Christ be dying and rising in my life at the same time? It is difficult to allow apparently contradictory truths to occupy equal space in our hearts. We grow anxious and impatient. We attempt to force resolution one way or another. We issue ultimatums and threats.

Implicit in such thinking may be the assumption that somewhere hanging out in the ether is truth—truth, objective and obvious, provable and as certain as the pear tree outside my window. Another assumption may be that truth resonates subjectively in my own experience and conscience, and that they are the only ultimate authority. Hence we may turn to our opponent with the condescending attitude that "if you were not so sinful or wounded or stupid you would see all this and agree with me."

Yet from my vantage point, truth shimmers and is multivalent. It dances and surprises like a good poem. It will not be stuffed in your back pocket but squirms out, oozes down your leg, and gets stuck on the sole of your shoe. You get home and start to peel it off and find half a dozen other things you picked up on the way. Truth gets the giggles and tap dances. It dresses up in gothic cathedrals and lies in the gutter on the bad side of town. We can come to know it, but we can never possess it. And its subversive agenda is the total occupation of our hearts.

I suppose we can set out to seek truth, to be truthful, but such enterprises are apt to be unsuccessful. Truth is not something we seize upon, but rather most often it leaps out from bushes in dark alleys when we are not looking and grabs us by the throat. It seizes us out of the clutches of misery or pride. Truth teases us in our dreams. It will not be manipulated, cogitated, or collated by human mind.

Jesus said he was it and that we would know it and it would set us free. Finally truth suffers disbelief, hurts, and dies. And in the end truth saves—on its terms, in its time.

OUT OF CONFLICT, polarization, mistrust, and impasse comes the invitation to turn one's attention away from the conflict to Jesus Christ. When we feel our most cherished beliefs are threatened, there is a natural tendency to shore up our position with proofs of various kinds. We want to be right. We want to be vindicated from the criticism and attack of our enemies. Yet as we are willing to surrender our opinions and look to Jesus to be the reconciler in periods of conflict, we can be led into deeper trust and fellowship with God.

Such surrender requires us to tolerate ambiguity and to wrestle with what is truth and how we know what we know. We begin to discover what is authoritative for us and what is not. We accept responsibility not for possessing truth but for entering into relationship with it, as it reigns in the perplexing, seemingly irreconcilable realm of our opposing positions.

At the conclusion of a conference on spirituality and the Church, a young woman from the East Coast was up most of the night praying for the Church and its conflicts. Toward dawn she turned to this passage from Isaiah:

> Enlarge the site of your tent,/and let the curtains of your habitation be stretched out;/do not hold back; lengthen your cords/and strengthen your stakes./For you will spread out to the right and to the left,/and your descendants will possess the nations and settle the desolate towns.
>
> Do not fear, for you will not be ashamed;/do not be discouraged, for you will not suffer disgrace;/for you will forget the shame of your youth,/and the disgrace of your widowhood you will remember no more. (54:2-4)

It is not up to us to reconcile the contradictions between others and ourselves. Our tent can be large enough to accommodate opposing truths without negating our own. Rather, our task is to articulate, with all the freedom, clarity, and joy we can muster, the way we see things. We are neither judge nor jury but witnesses to life's trial. The bloody struggle for personal truth-telling is part of the labor of prayer. A glad compelling witness is the fruit.

CHAPTER 23

The Star Stopped
Joy: Our Chief and Highest End

When they had heard the king, they set out; and there, ahead of them, went the star that they had seen at its rising, until it stopped over the place where the child was. When they saw that the star had stopped they were overwhelmed with joy.

— MATTHEW 2:9–10

The star stopped.

Did they slam into one another like dominoes—camels, gifts, and magi all in a scrambled pile before the manger? They had been seeking joy for so long; and they knew more about traveling than arriving, more about need than fulfillment.

The star stopped. The momentum of the journey and the habit of search sent us lurching forward even as we beheld the prize. Like travelers on a long auto trip over the flat stretch of prairie, we lie still at night in our beds feeling ourselves hurtling along phantom highways, our flesh imprinted to motion.

So we arrive, yet we act as if we are still on the way. We shuffle on unsteady legs to the doorway where the light glows and the breath of cattle steams, and something makes a low choking coo, and we are overwhelmed with joy, a sublime apprehension of the beauty and perfection of what lies before us under the stars.

It doesn't get any better than this:

the glad dog bounding gleefully after the yellow cat in the sun

curled leaves lying like crisp fists under the maple

clutter in the child's room—a still swirl of hairbrushes, dirty socks, ribbons, Tootsie Rolls, and crayons

you and your friend laughing over lunch in the cozy diner.

You think you need to get busy, accomplish something today. Wild-eyed John in his camel's hair is out in the pasture yelling to get with it. "Bear fruit worthy of repentance, you brood of vipers," he shouts (Matt. 3:7, 8). There is so much to do, so far to go. You think this thing or that thing has to be done. You think joy is up ahead, when you have reached some goal, satisfied that hunger.

We ought not to pray for things, but to pray to live as though we had the things we pray for. We ought to discover just what we think these things will give us, to consider carefully what is the subtext of our desire.

The star stopped. Did they pile into each other like keystone cops? Was a screeching cosmic brake applied? Or was it so silent it was hardly noticed in the din of rising galaxies and earth teeming with the shrill frenzy of life and death? Perhaps there was a gentle slowing pressure in the heart, an impulse to do something unfamiliar, maybe a sudden press upon the shoulders to bend the knees and halt midway down the stairs absorbed in joy.

The star stopped and cast its radiance like a neon arrow: *Exit now. Food. Gas. Lodging.*

HERE THIS IS IT. You need go no further. The star stopped, and they were overwhelmed with joy. Well, how long did that last? How long before they began to fret, to glance anxiously at their watches and their bank balance, and to worry about the future? How long before Herod and their disturbing dreams intruded? Back home, how were they going to explain the dishes still undone, the laundry piled upon the floor, the unpaid bills?

And afterwards, how long would it be before they began to doubt their own eyes—that they really had seen what they had seen? "Perhaps I was mistaken, it all seems so unreal. It was long ago. I was ill, or grieving, or young and foolish. We'd better keep on looking, just in case."

O immaculate tenderness, O sweet hay in the wind, ground of our beseeching, joy of our desiring, we meet and greet you, kneel to adore and leave our gifts, then what? You are too much for us—you in your completeness, sufficiency. We, overwhelmed with joy, cannot bear the light and back out of the radiant stable to return to the familiar world of anxious fear and endless seeking.

The tension of incompletion fuels our lives and impels our action. Consummation is hard to take. People shouldn't be so happy. "I'm sorry, Mom, but I just can't keep my smiles down," confides Cicelia apologetically on her eagerly awaited trip to the ice-skating rink.

If we get too satisfied, won't there be no striving, no invention, no creativity, and no urge to improve, discover, and move on? Won't it be boring? Won't it be dull? Our capacity for satisfaction is much less than our capacity for hunger. Who dares to take a vow of stability? Who dares declare that this is it—this broken-down stable of a life—and that this very life in shambles shelters joy?

What most characterizes American culture, poet Richard Wilbur has said, "is not unity, but rather a disjunction and incoherence aggravated by an intolerable rate of change."[27] I gaze in bewildered nostalgia at old photographs of loved ones and myself. Motion is an essential property of things. Everything at one level of its being or another is in motion and change. Is anything in the universe absolutely still? The earth heaves, crumbles, splits, and powders. The flesh pulses, sighs, and dies in the slow dance of decay. Electrons career around nuclei. Five-flavored quarks flash in kinetic quickstep.

A lot depends on the way the willow leaf turns in the wind and curls to a dry crisp under the bird feeder, but even more depends on someone's stopping to notice. Our awareness gives birth to Christ. Seeing that the star has stopped and then climbing down from the camel to kneel before the Holy Child dwelling in the heart of matter with innocence and salvation is what opens the door for God's entry into our world. The Child yearns to be noticed. The Child waits in the crib of creation for us to stop and pick it up and deliver it to the world by virtue of our own seeing. Christ is born by our consent. It all depends on someone's saying, "Let it be to me according to thy word." Then a still, small soul magnifies the Holy One and, like a mirrored prism, bends light into multicolored beams of joy.

THERE WAS A MAN who played with Jesus a kind of peek-a-boo and hide-and-seek, asking to see him while he walked. I go now where the man prayed, and Jesus is everywhere, sitting in the trees, hanging upside down from the hawk's nest, swinging his arms up ahead along the cow path, turning in wide circles in the heavens, glinting under the silver wings of geese. "Jesus, get out of here," I say. "I have work to do, prayers to pray, fears to nurture, pain to bear, miles to go before I sleep."

He just grins, riding down the back of the willow leaf. "You bet," he says, "who do you think is in charge here anyway? I came that you might have life abundant."

"Yes, but there is so much suffering and sorrow in the world. I have survivor's guilt."

"Bear up, Sweetheart, that comes with salvation." Then he quotes Scripture: "'Do not be like a horse or a mule without understanding,/whose temper must be curbed with bit and bridle,/or else it will not stay near you' (Ps. 32:9). Daughter, your father forgives you for being happier than he. In your joy is his joy completed."

> "What is the chief and highest end of humankind?" asks the Larger Catechism. "Humankind's chief and highest end is to glorify God and to fully enjoy God." [28]

A FRIEND OF MINE died recently after a long, debilitating illness. Before he died he told me, "Life is funny. You know, I used to say life is messy. Now I say life is funny. God must be laughing his head off at us, saying, 'Don't they get it?' I have no complaints. Life has been very good to me. I just try to enjoy."

To enjoy means to put into a state of or to be in joy—to indwell rejoicing. Joy is the emotion provoked by well-being, success, or possessing what one desires. How strange that little teaching in the Church has to do with helping us to be faithful to our highest end. We know how to read and interpret Scripture. We understand the dynamics of church growth. We can conduct things decently and in order. We can do mission. We are even beginning to understand our spiritual life and prayer. But how many of us can state precisely how it is we glorify and enjoy God as individuals and as a community of faith? When many of us start to enjoy, we feel guilty. To claim that anything I might do actually glorifies God may sound arrogant. To seek enjoyment of God seems hedonistic, wrong.

It takes courage to risk joy. The older we get, the more we know of the ravages of life and sin, and the woeful limitations of the flesh. My dying friend, weak and suffering, says, "I just try to enjoy." Perhaps that is when joy is born most truly—when we are firmly fixed in the limits of humanity, held by the teeth of our extremity with no illusions. Maybe you won't get better. Maybe your friend will die. Maybe your heart will be broken. Maybe the divorce will be final. Maybe the worse that can happen will happen. Now here, just when you thought it was all over, here, stop where the star has stopped and let joy in. It will take a mile if you give it an inch—easing a hand and foot through the crack, pushing in a shoulder and hip, and flinging the door wide open on bliss. What did you think would make the star stop, if not the sad song of mortal need?

A LOT DEPENDS on the way the yellow willow leaf swims like a slim minnow downstream to rest in the musty shallows of earth. Now it turns, spins in circles, now it dips and glides, now stops, still in the air, then drops like a sigh. A lot depends on such surrender, but even more depends on someone noticing.

> *Jesus, help us to love you*
> *more than the search for you.*
> *Give us hearts of merriment and gratitude.*
> *Teach us to tolerate goodness, to stable delight.*
> *And, Merciful Savior of loss and defeat,*
> *bestow upon us the wit to trust*
> *and to consent to contentment*
> *that your joy and our joy be made complete.*

CHAPTER 24

I'm an Inside Dog
Union with God the Father

*A*hs strains his head through the wire gate to his pen, looking toward the house and pleading, "Arf. Arf. Arf. I'm out here. You're in there. Surely there has been a mistake. Arf. Arf. Arf." Over and over he barks with increasing alarm and irritating intensity. Then abruptly he withdraws his head, trots back in his house, and sits on the beat-up couch his master bought at a yard sale.

The dog appears to be confused. He wants to live in the house like the humans. My friend counsels emphatically, "This dog of yours is very neurotic."

Recently, in a simultaneous show of authority and bad taste, Ahs bit our visiting pastor on the right buttock. He does this not to strangers and potential thieves but to people we like, to anybody who might compete for what he perceives as the limited amount of affection from the two large creatures who lead the pack.

Ahs's confusion is our fault, I guess, for treating him too much like a human, for rolling on the floor with him and playing like puppies ourselves, for projecting onto him our unconscious needs and wishes. In significant ways, of course, dogs are not at all like humans. Take rolling in manure, for instance. Most humans do not find that satisfying. Ahs comes home wearing *Au du Poop* on his neck like an exotic perfume. The fragrances tell where he has been, what he has seen, and who has been through the neighborhood.

AND WHO ARE WE? Are we any less confused than Ahs? Are we spiritual beings trying to become human, as some maintain, or are we human beings trying to become spiritual? The question may also express God's dilemma—coming to earth, entering our world, taking on the flesh. Jesus never could wipe off that scent of sanctity around his collar. People could tell he'd been places they had never been. He wore the odor of righteousness like a pleasing

113

offering. The crowd pressed in around him seeking to get a whiff of the truth, a little aromatherapy for the soul.

Some of us may treat Jesus as we do our pets. We smother him with our projections and needs. Or we infantilize him into a pampered domesticated Jesus who suits us. Or we dispatch him to the outer reaches of our lives in a distant pen and stop by occasionally to drop a little something in his plate and scratch his ears.

Many assumptions Christians have accepted about the Church, culture, and Christ are being challenged these days. Some people labor to separate the Jesus of dogma and the Jesus of the Church with its politics and squabbles from the "historical Jesus." Others preach "Jesus" and claim they present the authentic Christ.

The one I put my money on to redeem Christianity for contemporary culture is Jesus himself—although, Lord knows, there are a lot of things about him that are hard to take. For example, there is his exasperating and politically incorrect exclusivity, "I and the Father are one. No one comes to the Father, but by me." How can that be? What on earth does he mean by that?

Well, for one thing, I think he means you'd better keep your eye on him, because, after all, the Lord thy God is a jealous God. And like Ahs, this jealous God is apt to bite your guests on the butt. Okay, maybe not your guests, but whatever you have invited into your life that you are putting before him. When this happens, it usually hurts a lot, because you lose a good chunk of what you have been sitting on to cushion yourself against the hard cold pew of life.

FROM THE START, Jesus was pretty clear about who he was, so clear, in fact, that it got him into trouble. "Who does he think he is?" people asked. "What gives him the right?" And they chased him out of town (Luke 4:28-29).

Jesus heard the Creator, the Authenticating Source, identify him as "my son, my beloved, the one who pleases me well." This was Jesus' self-identity, who he thought he was. Such self-understanding released and empowered his ministry.

As we grow in faith and put on the mind of Christ, we begin to know and appreciate who he thinks he is; and then who we think we are begins to change as we are transformed by this renewing of our minds and enter into Christ's consciousness. We begin to see the world as he sees it, through his eyes. Deeper union leads to participating in Jesus' consciousness of himself.

A significant part of Jesus' self-consciousness was how he understood his relationship with God. *I and the Father are one.* It was Jesus' cherished prayer that we might enjoy the same union with Authoritative Power as he did.

> As you, Father, are in me and I am in you, may they also be in us. So that the world may believe that you have sent me . . . I made your name known to them, and I will make it known, so that the love with which you have loved me may be in them, and I in them. (John 17:21, 26)

Jesus saw such an intimate relationship with God as possible for each of us. Taking up the cross and following Jesus to Jerusalem is not an end in itself. It is what must happen for us to see and let go of our false selves and discover in ourselves the love, authoritative power, and abundance of the Father. Basil Pennington describes the false self as made of "what I do, what I have, and what others think of me. This is the self Jesus said must die so that our true self can emerge."[29]

How does this union with God the Father happen for us? In part through the crucifixion of our holy child, our sacred self at the hands of the lesser fathers and the false self.

It is crucifying to an individual and a culture when fathers do not act like fathers—when they do not speak with authority, with personal integrity, with a respect for their ability to bless and curse by their word alone, when they do not take responsibility to protect holiness and provide abundance.

From education to government, commerce to the Church, the institutions and structures of the culture, which once held value and meaning, have been exposed in their inevitable limitation and sin. We have many fallen fathers and little trust in public figures. There is a pervasive sense of mistrust, nihilism, and anger. Cynicism has replaced hope. Self-pity and opportunism have replaced altruism. We are miserly with the grace and forgiveness we extend to others and ourselves. What was promised, what we thought we had a right to, have been denied. We look around for someone to blame and spend a good deal of time biting our pastors, politicians, and other leaders.

In the random violence of our cities, in the voices of the fifty-one percent of our children who live without both their biological parents, in the increasing disparity between the rich and the poor, we cry out, "Father, why hast thou forsaken me?" Here, *father* may be my literal father or any of a number of other fathers: my church, my college degree, my wife, my country, my job, my good looks. *Father* may be whatever it is in which I have placed my hope and expectation of self-validation, which has had ultimate authority in my life. "Father, why hast thou forsaken us?" We are abandoned, humiliated, crucified.

That's the cross. Here is where a good many find themselves these days, impaled on broken dreams. Here is the resurrection: I am raised to new life, as I relate with welcoming forgiveness, love, and protection, to the part of myself that is childlike, vulnerable, and holy and has been betrayed by some lesser father. Through this redemptive act, *who I think I am* expands to include *Father*.

I become one with Christ Jesus—whom we might describe as the sufficiency of the flesh, the incarnate sanctity of my particularity—through my suffering. I am raised with him as I discover my union with the Father, the one who begets this fragile flesh.

JESUS SAYS no one comes to such union except by him, except, we might say, through the identification of the self with the suffering God, so that my story becomes God's story and God's story becomes my story. This is the story of holiness seeking to give itself in love to creation, holiness seeking to be believed and accepted, holiness shamed and violated, and holiness redeemed and given new life.

It takes a crucifixion for us to love what God loved first. As holiness suffers, it is finally recognized for what it is. We say with the astonished centurion, "Truly this man was God's son!" Truly I am a self of infinite value and worth! As I am diminished by the losses of life, the reality of God in me may be increased and appreciated through my grief and suffering. For pain often speaks more convincingly of our divine heritage than mere possession of it.

In the journey with Jesus I come to love and forgive what I despise in others and myself. I am healed of my self-contempt, shame, and blame as I surrender to Christ and simultaneously to the ragged truth about myself. My *I* begins to be Christ's *I*. His Father becomes my Father as I discover the Father in me, doing and being for myself what I have been asking external things to do for me, namely, to protect, approve, and give me authority.

When I am one with God the Father, I have stopped looking for father out there or up there and discovered that father and all that father means is alive in me, is intimately one with me and that this somehow has been accomplished through the mystery of my journey with the Son of God to the cross and beyond.

Then the gulf between me and the power and grace that I need to sustain myself, which was so difficult for me to access on my own, has been bridged. The redeemer and the redeemed are one. In the words of St. Augustine, "My life will be a real life, being wholly full of Thee."[30]

In Jesus, God breaks out of the confines of heaven, leaps over the celestial gate, and comes inside with us, saying, "You, too, are my only child, my beloved. You, too, are pleasing to me."

CHAPTER 25 ✓

Boredom and Vulnerability
The Search for the Historical Jesus

*B*utterscotch, our golden rabbit, and the venerable dog, Ahs, reclined in the shade under the pear tree. A gentle breeze lifted the hair on their necks. Butterscotch, safe in her cage, stretched her hind legs out behind her stubby tail. Ahs lay with his chin on the ground, nose close to the cage, eyes watchful. He heaved a long sigh.

"Stinky Dog, it is rude for you to drool like that when you look at me," Butterscotch said. "Don't think for a minute that I don't notice how your jaw goes slack and you begin to salivate every time you see me. A prey species never has a moment's rest. Which is why I say Jesus is getting a bad rap. Folks sniffing him up one side and down the other, running circles around him, chasing him into the brush, cornering him with their philosophies and theologies, poking him with their politics, trapping him in their minds—like he was some wild thing somebody wanted to make a hat or mittens out of."

The dog sighed again. "How do you know he doesn't like it?" he asked. "Maybe he even brought it all about."

The rabbit pointedly rubbed her nose with her paw. Carnivores have terrible breath. "Well, if you really knew him as I do, you'd see my point," she sniffed.

The topic for the afternoon was epistemology—truth, and how you know what you know. Specifically, the two creatures were discussing the quest for the historical Jesus, the search by biblical scholars to determine the historical reliability of the Gospels. Some see their findings as a frontal attack on Christianity.

Not that the rabbit put much store in two-legged saviors; but she was able to recognize truth when she saw it. Ahs, on the other hand, slavishly worshiped two-leggeds, followed them about, whined and begged to eat their food, and lay next to them. Butterscotch knew for a fact that Ahs let them pet him and never cleaned up afterward.

Since the pair could not read, they hadn't gotten as far as taking votes on whether Jesus really said and did the things that Scripture claimed. Besides, the sun was warm on their backs and the wind just right to waft the fragrance of honeysuckle their way. And neither believed that the veracity of scriptural witness was the real issue.

How does one know what one knows? On what do we base our hope? On what authority does one make a claim? And just what does *real* mean anyway? Butterscotch, like the man born blind in John's Gospel, rested her case on the indisputable facts of her experience: "I do not know whether he is a sinner. One thing I know, that once I was blind, now I see!" (John 9:25). Ahs, on the other hand, more faithful or more gullible, relied on the testimony of tradition and the dogma of the Church. The Apostles' Creed was good enough for him.

Each, though, appreciated the limitations of his or her perspective. Neither the uncritical acceptance of systematic dogmatics nor the subjective witness of the inner bunny could completely satisfy the inquiring mind. In the end the two were left with the disquieting notion that everything might be in the eye of the beholder, the universe a dream, and the two of them, snoozing under the pear tree, only the imagination of some mind larger than their own.

THERE IS A BIT of the scientist in anyone who sets out to test in his or her own life if Jesus Christ is really all he is cracked up to be. "Prove it," the contemplative says to God. Here are all these promises: freedom, joy, abundance, peace, wholeness, justice, truth, and life eternal. "Show me," says the contemplative, setting out to experiment with divinity in the laboratory of experience.

In the beginning, God is the object of the search. But at some point God may peremptorily rise out of the test tube and take over the experiment. I find myself being dissected. My soul is flayed open by truth. I am blinded by glaring light and toasted over a Bunsen burner, where my impurities are burned away and I am distilled into my essence. I am no longer in control of this process. The knower and the known have shifted places. And truth is not something I can find, but something that has me in its grasp.

THEOLOGIAN Lesslie Newbigin observes, "Reason, even the most acutely critical reason, cannot establish truth. . . . [This is because] you cannot criticize a statement of what claims to be the truth except on the basis of some other truth-claim which—at the moment—you accept without criticism. But that truth-claim on which your critique is based must in turn be criticized. . . . Any claim to know truth is, therefore, simply a concealed assertion of power."[31]

The work of scientist Michael Polanyi reminds us that "all knowing involves the personal participation of the knower, that knowing always involves the risk of being wrong, and that the struggle to know calls for the fullest exercise of personal responsibility."[32]

Ultimately, though, instead of seeking proofs of God from reason or experience, the contemplative finds fulfillment simply and humbly dwelling in love in God's presence. The contemplative gives God entry into the world not through a claim of truth but through a believing heart. Instead of an exercise of power through the assertion of one's own reality over another's via dazzling argument or feats of spiritual prowess, the contemplative takes the vulnerable route of allowing God to make God's own appeal through the context of his or her surrendered life.

I acknowledge my vulnerability when I say, "I cannot know it all. I may be wrong. This is what I see. This is what I am responsible for articulating as clearly as I can." We might characterize the spiritual journey as the process of discovering right relationship to this vulnerability, which we meet in ourselves, in others, and in God.

Vulnerability is the capacity to be wounded and wronged, open to attack or damage. Our vulnerability may include our sin and temptation to evil, our failure and weakness—wherever we are not whole, wherever we fall short of the glory that is our promised inheritance as God's children.

We can relate to our woundedness in many ways: with anger, resentment, impatience, contempt, deceit, shame, and blame. We can so identify ourselves with our vulnerability that we know ourselves only as victim. Then, committed to our suffering and stubbornly resistant to healing, we may defend our wounds with fierce loyalty.

God sends into our consciousness, into the heart of matter, Holy Vulnerability in the form of Jesus. It teaches, heals, suffers, dies, and rises saying, "Look, watch me. This is what it means to be human. It is all right. Everyone is wounded. Follow me and be healed."

Over and over Jesus' ministry reached out to the vulnerable ones. He brought home the lost and the misfits saying, "You belong, too." He didn't bring them back to turn them into Jews or folks like him. He just brought them back saying, "You, just as you are, are important. You have a contribution to make. We need you. You belong."

Loving Jesus takes away our shame for being human as nothing else can. For he shows us how to be poor, how to value and appreciate our vulnerability. He tells us the vulnerable ones will see God and inherit the kingdom of heaven. He helps us get off our high horse and come down where we ought to be, on our knees.

In the painful encounter with our vulnerability and diminishment, we meet the diminished, suffering God and our own holiness. For in my poverty, I discover my true worth. Stripped of what I can do, what I possess, how I am known by others—all the external ways I have attempted to create worth for myself—I find my true self in the center of my humility, which is also the dwelling place of the Trinity.

I used to read my children a story about a little girl who was born with a long tail like a dragon. Various characters seek to help the child with what is perceived by some as her disability. I liked Mike the cat's approach best: "Teach her to love her tail," he sagely advised. He shows the girl how to switch her tail back and forth, wind it around the fire escape railing, and hang upside down. *Teach her to love her tail.*

Part of the task of the Church is to teach us to love our tails and God's tail, Jesus. Spirituality without Jesus Christ is spirituality that may be resisting the fundamental truth of our vulnerability. It may be a spirituality that, well- or ill-disguised, is exercising power, trying to be God.

THE WORLD HOLDS vulnerability with fear and contempt. The Church ought to teach us to hold it in our arms and love it. But the Church is, of course, vulnerable, too.

I was trying on a new hat when eleven-year-old Cicelia observed that you should always wear a hat to church. "It protects you from boredom, Mom. The boredom rays, like the ultraviolet rays from the sun, are in church and sometimes at school. If you have on a hat, you will be protected from the boredom."

I hope the place where you worship is not boring. Maybe if churches had more to do with being with God and less to do with talking about God, things wouldn't be so boring for Cicelia and others. For as Evelyn Underhill observed, "God is the interesting thing."[33] A good deal of church seems to have little to do with God and is conducted as though God were, if not absent, at least very far away. Little time is given for God to get a word in edgewise. Our frantic activity and anxious busyness demonstrate our faithless creed that not much of anything can happen without our doing it ourselves.

Perhaps more conscious attention to God in worship is just too risky, too frightening. What if nothing happens? What if nothing is changed or accomplished? Once Cicelia put a sign on her door painted in large red letters:

KNOK or ELSE!

Red paint ominously dripped from the letters like blood. Jesus, we know you stand at the door and knock, but beware! We resist transformation. Devoted to our losses and the sins of others against us, we do not really trust your power in our lives.

The Church will always be imperfect. It will be unimaginative and boring and rigid sometimes, because we are unimaginative and boring and rigid sometimes. Thank goodness God's presence doesn't depend on our winning academy awards in best Pentecost service of the year.

I have been in so many churches where I wonder why anybody comes at all. What with the dozen dusty arrangements of silk flowers and the sappy pictures of Jesus and the bad skating-rink-organ-music, I don't know what the appeal could be. The appeal, of course, is Jesus. Jesus is there and active, because the people believe in him. Their vulnerable belief holds the door open for the vulnerable God to enter.

BUTTERSCOTCH WENT to church a couple of times. Once was on Easter in the degrading role of a visual aid for the children's sermon. The other time was the annual outdoor service held at the lake. She hopped about on her leash, nibbling clover among the lawn chairs while the people sang and prayed. When the pastor began the communion prayer, she got her leash caught between her toes, and her attempts to free herself only drove the leash tighter into her tender flesh. Just as the pastor was getting into the meat of the Great Thanksgiving, Butterscotch began a series of loud piercing shrieks. "Eee! Eee! Eee!" she screamed. Her mistresses pulled on her leash, increasing her pain. "Eee! Eee! Eee!" Had something bitten her or someone stepped on her? Was she going to die in agony in front of us all? The pastor valiantly pronounced the Words of Institution. The children scrambled to the rabbit's aid and drew the leash from between her scraped, raw toes. That Sunday Cicelia said that church was not boring.

As for Butterscotch, she has no intention of ever returning to church. She finds it difficult to find a common ground with a species that eats what it claims it adores.

According to the rabbit, anybody who noses around trying to figure out exactly what Jesus did or did not say and keeps fooling around with spirituality without Jesus simply doesn't know Jesus, hasn't a clue as to who he is.

"Stinky Dog," she said, "take me for instance. When the two-leggeds hold me and I snuggle up under their chins and lick their fingers and lie still on their laps, when they feel my soft fur, when I soak up their sadness and weariness and alienation, when they look in my eyes and our souls connect, when they hold in their hands the pulse of sweet vulnerability, does it matter where I came from or what I think about myself? When they stop thinking *about* me and are just *with* me, there is only love."

Ahs just sighed and scratched his ear. "No," he thought idly to himself, "there is only lunch."

Jesus—lunch or love? To the one who satisfies our deepest hunger, there may not be much difference.

CHAPTER 26

I Want! I Need! I Have to Have!
The Taming of Desire

The door slams shut. "Hi, Mom! I'm home." Gym bag, shoes, trumpet case, thud on the carpet. "I want something to eat. I need a new backpack. I have to have a blue folder for English.

"I want to have someone spend the night. I need new shoes for cross-country. I have to have a lyre for my flute. I want my own phone! I need new jeans. I have to have that green glitter nail polish.

"I want Cicelia to stay out of my room! I need roller blades. I have to have contacts before class pictures."

I want—I need—I have to have: a writhing nest of seething desires snaking in and out of awareness.

*S*ummoned by command of the merest wish, the capacity to will serves first to make us conscious of what we do not have and then to give us the determination to get it. Volition, the precious power to will, is necessary to our very existence. Volition draws us into relationships, work, and meaning. It flows out of our awareness of lack, of not possessing something we value, and impels us into the world of action where we meet our needs.

Desire gives me identity, as it sings its song in me. What I am attracted to—*what I want and need and have to have*—gives me form and definition. My desire, reaching out into creation like so many eager arms taking back into itself what it deems worthy, reflects my particular preferences, inclinations, and loves. I long to incorporate into myself what I desire. Why? Perhaps to soothe the anxiety of being human, of being essentially alone and free.

Maybe to comfort, to give me a sense of power, protection, and ease. And most certainly, to keep me alive.

I project onto the object of my desire what I experience as lacking in myself. What is incomplete or unrecognized in me, I may see in my beloved. I may endow the beloved with what I perceive to be my deficiencies. Then I yearn to possess the beloved as the key to my wholeness.

THE ANGLICAN PRIEST and founder of contemplative communities in India and Hong Kong, who gave me advice as I began this ministry of prayer, once told me, "If you can avoid it, don't own anything. If you own things, you will have to take care of them, and that will take away from your prayer."

Once one of the friars with St. Francis asked if he might own just one book. Francis replied, "No, if you have a book, you will begin to feel self-important, and then you will ask another brother to fetch it for you." This familiar "Breviary Story" illustrates Francis's awareness of how possessions may lead to self-importance and self-importance to exploitation of others.

ONE DESIRE LEADS to another, and before you know it, in the words of Pedro Arrupe, "The superfluous becomes the convenient; the convenient becomes the necessary; the necessary becomes the indispensable." Arrupe, speaking at the Third World Congress, observed that "an enormous percentage of men and women who live in countries that abound in material goods seem to have changed the name of our species from homo sapiens to homo consumens. From infancy we are sculpted and shaped into consumers by the hand of advertising which is now like the air we breath."[34]

MUCH OF THE spiritual journey has to do with the education or training of our desire. Like a wild horse, the will must be subdued before it can serve us well. I want! I need! I have to have! The will bucks and kicks, seeks to shrug off any controls upon it while we watch shaking our heads at its power and independence. "I can will what is right, but I cannot do it. For I do not do the good I want, but the evil I do not want is what I do," anguishes St. Paul (Rom. 7:18–19).

Saint John of the Cross compares the development of the soul to a child who is slowly weaned from the breast of God's love to mature faith. This is the substantial faith called solid food.

The writer of Hebrews advises that this solid food is "reserved for those whose faculties have been trained by practice to distinguish good from evil" (5:14).

The training process of taming and weaning is painful. Our own resistance may create some of the pain. We sit at the table prepared for us kicking our feet, stubbornly refusing to eat the broccoli and green beans, demanding ice cream and milk shakes. Like a patient parent, God listens to our fuss—yet quietly imposes boundaries necessary to our well-being.

THERE ARE MOMENTS in prayer when we may sense something of the power of the divine will moving through us into the world like a thick stream of molten gold. This divine leaning into creation is so heavy it sits us down, kneels us down. The Author of All Longing and Desire, the Heart of Hunger, presses down into us with awesome, immense urgency. God's will seeks access into creation through our wills. The greater the freedom and spaciousness we bring to our wills, the greater the power of redeeming love that may move through us into the groaning creation.

Most of our energies involve strengthening and affirming the individual will and binding it to our purposes rather than freeing it for supple service to the Creator. Through the transformation of our minds in Christ, our wills are gradually conformed to the divine will. The internal conflict and painful tension between my will and God's will, which has left me stressed out, guilty, ineffective, and joyless, is resolved in the marriage of my will to God's. I discover, to my amazement, that what God wants is what I want, that God's beloved is also my beloved.

We can be grateful that God is in charge of this process, because there is little in the world to help us accomplish such selflessness. I recently saw a full-page newspaper ad for a seminar on how to be a success. "How much you earn is determined by how much you learn," trumpeted the ad. The daylong event boasted "live and in person" motivational experts from the worlds of business, sports, science, government, entertainment, and, yes, even religion. A special bonus in small print was the optional fifteen-minute session on the biblical secrets of success.

Testimonials oozed, "You can never be rich enough or thin enough or successful enough. You can never get enough motivation. If I can apply 1/10 of what I picked up today, I will double my income."

In a culture where every need must be met, every hunger satisfied, how can the Church offer sanctuary and help to ones who want to be weaned from their consuming addictions? It is all too easy for the Church and its institutions to become caught in the snares of consumption and worship the idol of success.

Yet, in the words of Jesus scholar John Dominic Crossan, "We've been told by God quite clearly that, I don't want your worship unless it is the symbolic face of justice. I don't want your Eucharist unless it tells quite clearly that I come to you as food and it is equal to all. Nobody gets a bigger host than somebody else."[35]

I ONCE READ of a saintly woman who lived on one communion wafer a day. She found her life literally in the body of Christ. Her meat and drink was the will of God. When a soul comes up against something it deeply desires and encounters refusal, real spiritual work begins. What the person wants may appear on the surface to be right, good, surely in accordance with God's plan. Yet the soul continues to meet frustration. Such frustration can push us into honest examination of our consciences. We are invited to look more closely at our motives. Why do I want this thing so much? What do I think I will gain from it? I may be making my happiness contingent on achieving a particular response from the world. What is exposed in my frustration is how I am more dependent on the world for my well being than on God. I am seeking my sustenance from some place other than the bread of Christ.

How can surrendering something I want very much be a way to life? How can denial of myself lead anywhere but to masochistic codependency and psychological damage? What good can come from the acceptance of personal suffering and loss? These are questions Jesus must surely have wrestled with in the Garden of Gethsemane.

In the end, all of Jesus' worldly success and accomplishments—the crowds, the brilliant teaching and preaching, the wonderful stories and parables, the spell-binding miracles, the dancing lame and obedient demons, even a dead man stumbling out of his tomb—all of that counted for little. What mattered then and now was the cross. Through his suffering, death, and resurrection, Jesus shows us the way to life. From the cross he whispers, "I will give up something most precious to me, something I have a right to, out of love for you, that you may be healed."

We have a right to well-being and success, to health, wealth, and the satisfaction of our needs. Yet when someone voluntarily surrenders that right, something is redressed or rectified in the economy of the realm of God. As I release my grip on my loaf of bread, someone else gets a fair share of the feast.

I give up my will to God. I offer myself to be a bearer of God's greater desire in the space made available by the surrender of my needs. My heart is no longer clogged and cramped by envy, craving, and self-seeking. Evil is overcome with good. Each time we voluntarily give up our will for our personal desires out of faith in and love for the larger good, mercy and redeeming life stream into the earth.

The less I look to the world to meet my needs, the freer I become to respond to it with healing power and compassion. There is a law of spiritual ethics at work here, similar to the boundaries observed in professional relationships. The ethical caregiver does not compromise the relationship by seeking to get his or her own needs met by the client. The caregiver has other places where personal needs are met. In a larger sense, we offer creation a freer, more powerful presence, as we do not seek to get our needs met by it but seek, rather, to serve it. We are set free to serve God's creation because we are not on its payroll. We are getting our supper at the table of Christ Jesus.

I do not know if the Church or any community can teach us how to do such a thing. For I suspect the transformation of the will occurs in the solitary encounter with God in the garden of suffering. It is by its nature a personal decision forged in the agony of individual life circumstances. Others may stand by, watch or sleep, judge or encourage, or even serve as examples. But the decision is made alone in the freedom of an individual conscience.

Such sacrifice is, in the literal sense of the word, holy work, a sacred deed. It begins with gratitude for one's privilege and thanksgiving for the blessings in one's life. It requires sensitivity to injustice, evil, and suffering, and a deep, abiding love for God and neighbor. The struggle is between your will for the thing your heart desires, your beloved (what it is you think will give you life and joy), and your desire for the healing and wholeness of another.

Through God's grace your eyes are opened to behold God's beloved as your beloved. What I want and need and have to have, and what God wants and needs and has to have, become the same.

The realm of God comes as we discover our beloved in the faces of the suffering ones on this planet, and as we choose to lay down our lives for them. Greater love has no one than this. *Thy kingdom come. Thy will be done.*

PART VI

· · ·

Becoming Ordinary

$\mathscr{I}$ began to settle down. For a number of years I had attempted to find validation for my prayer ministry externally. I wrote impassioned letters to denominational officials asking for help and support. I missed the fellowship and growth available in a community, although I still sensed my primary call to be to solitude. I thought that a community of prayer might give me encouragement, accountability, and protection.

I see the structures of the Church existing in part to serve as protective boundaries for the spiritual journey. I thought it was unwise, even dangerous, to pray and teach as I was doing without the shelter of a local church. At the same time, I did not want to create another para-church organization, which would then need to sustain itself.

I did meet regularly with a spiritual director and received supervision for my work with persons who came to me for spiritual guidance. I led weekly services of healing and offered pastoral care in a nearby hospital. I continued to hope I might find a church or religious community with which I could affiliate. Most of the churches I knew were concerned with survival, evangelism, retooling to attract Generations X and Y. I was a puzzling anachronism for many churchgoers.

The question I brought as I began this ministry was, What difference will this ministry make to the poorest person in the world? Now the question shifted and expanded to include, What difference will the poorest person in the world make to this ministry? This came about as I began to look to the poor, churched or unchurched, for my community. And with this understanding I got over some of my arrogance and grandiosity as I began to experience my ministry, my prayer, and myself as blessedly ordinary.

One day I was complaining to a friend about the frustrations I was experiencing, and she asked me, "What do you need in order to sustain you in this ministry?" At first I thought I wanted more funding, then I thought I wanted validation, but a couple weeks later I spontaneously told my friend, "What I need is a community that will support me in becoming poorer." What I meant was that I wanted accountability and help in deepening my spiritual poverty and in being faithful to a simple lifestyle.

The Church as a whole does not do that. Yet it is truly as I come up against my limitations, whether financial, spiritual, or physical, that I meet God. When I have nothing else to offer, then I am ready to offer Jesus.

So I continued to muddle along growing increasingly comfortable with things the way they were. I began to discover and more fully appreciate the informal network of support, wisdom, and prayer that had been sustaining me all along.

Here enter the animals. From the beginning, animals had figured in my journey, but now they began to show up more in my writing. And they were not content to simply add color and amusement, the dear things wanted to speak. The animals developed a following among some of my readers. The dog, cats, and rabbits even received occasional cards and inquiries. I seemed to have struck a chord.

What did whimsical animal fantasy have to do with spiritual formation? Did the creatures serve a purpose beyond a literary device and medium of revelation? I became curious about why animals held so much joy and interest for me and my readers. I think it is because animals naturally possess the poverty of spirit I was seeking for myself. Gerald Vann observed that the condition for happiness is a deep sense of our creatureliness.[36] I think part of becoming ordinary is the discovery and deep acceptance of the joy and freedom in our creatureliness. The animals help ground me and remind me that I, like them, am subject to One larger and greater than myself.

Contemplation, consolation, ecstacy, may have a tendency to inflate a person. Being entrusted with the spiritual care and nurture of others likewise may be inflating. The animals seemed to call me back to the earth, to simplicity, to surrender and trust.

> But ask the animals and they will teach you:
> the birds of the air, and they will tell you;
> ask the plants of the earth, and they will teach you;
> and the fish of the sea will declare to you.
>
> — JOB 12:7-8

Animals do not lie or pretend. They do not sin. They seem to know that God's omnipotence undergirds everything. Animals disarm our logical defenses and help us overcome our human resistance to grace. I even came to identify a state of being in myself I called "rabbit power." Rabbit power meant humility and the wisdom, balance, and earthy connectedness of an animal who lives as a prey species, close to the ground and mindful of its vulnerability. I connected rabbit power with taking off my shoes and walking barefoot. In my experience, no rabbit has ever appeared to pine after being something other than it is; rabbit power was a place where I could gratefully be who I am and therein find deep delight and peace.

Finally, communion with animals reflected my desire for union with God. To cross the chasm from one species to another and find communion and a sense of mutual respect and regard seemed to mirror my longing to connect with God. To establish a connection, an understanding, however slight, with something wholly other than oneself, is to participate in the eager groaning of a creation seeking wholeness and unity with its Creator.

Then one day, after complaining about wanting a community, I startled myself by saying, "My community is not of this world." Really? I wondered. My community is, for the most part, not of my immediate geographical setting, but rather far-flung. My community is also composed of the saints, whose writings have been so instructive and inspiring to me over the years. And though long unrecognized as such, my community also included Brother Dog, Sister Rabbit, and Mother Pear Tree.

One spring my husband and I were invited to a seminary as alumni-in-residence. We visited classes, spent time with students, and spoke with faculty. I was disturbed by the frantic state of many of the students I visited. At the faculty luncheon someone asked me what I thought they needed to do to respond effectively to a student body calling for more support in the areas of spiritual formation. The more I thought about it, the more impossible it seemed to me to do such a thing in the academic context. How can one insert a course on contemplation into a context in which most everything else is at odds with such an approach to ministry and the world?

Many seminaries and churches are institutions with a need to perpetu-ate themselves. They tend to regard poverty and vulnerability with fear. Prayer teaches us to hold poverty in our arms and tell it we love it. Much of what passes for the Church these days extols success, increase, and the ever-escalating accumulation of goods. I needed persons who could help me have the courage and strength to be downwardly mobile.

What I was seeking was an appreciation of something very few people understand and, in the end, something I had to give to myself. The work of prayer is hard, sacrificial, and demanding in many ways. As much as I want-ed to conceive of it otherwise, God has asked me to accept the constraints of a ministry that exists moment by moment out of God's grace. Over and over, the very lack of support or understanding sent me to that place of depend-ence on Christ's mercy where I seemed to do the most good. I now count it as a blessing that I did not always have the support I thought I wanted.

1996–1998

CHAPTER 27 ✳

Holy Ground and Squatter's Rights
Recollection: The Lasting Beauty of a Quiet Spirit

Let your adornment be the inner self with the lasting beauty of a gentle and quiet spirit, which is very precious in God's sight.

— 1 PETER 3:4

*W*inter came early that year. Eight inches of heavy, wet snow fell on leaves still green, weighing branches down to the ground in graceful arches until they cracked and split like gunshots in the startled autumn air. Later, after the sun came out, the trees hastened to spin green into gold and copper. Leaves scurried down to the earth, rushing to catch up to their appointment with death.

Butterscotch tucked her feet under her chin ruff and laid her ears back against her head. Everything about her was drawn in. She seemed to inhale herself into herself as she sat motionless simmering, gaining power and richness in the chill wind.

The Jewish mystic Isaac Luria spoke of God withdrawing like that and called it *tzimtzum*. God contracts, Luria said, in order to make room for the creation, which occurs by a beam of light from the infinite into the newly provided space. It is as though God pulls back, tucks in all that God is, and creates in the absence of the divine reality a sort of black hole—a dark velvet womb of mystery—out of which universes are born.

Butterscotch had absented herself and left behind a mound of soft golden fur. Her focus had shifted from watching the leaves scuttle across the deck and listening to the thud of pears hitting the ground to some inner ineffable rabbit realm. She was absolutely still. Time passed.

THE DEFINITION of recollection is quiet tranquility of mind and self-possession. Recollection is the gentle art of prayerful gathering-in in preparation for deeper prayer. One calls back the scattered, fragmented self, strewn about one's world like trash on a windy day. I pick up the pieces, sweep out the psychic debris, reorder the clutter, and bring back to the center—wholeness. All about me that is frantic and frayed, dispersed, helter-skelter, leaving me anxious, confused, and overwhelmed is drawn back. I am no longer like a cracked and broken bowl that leaks and spills its contents, but I am mended and suitable once again for holding my life, for containing safely and serviceably who I am.

In his sublime prayer for the church at Ephesus, Paul prays that God may grant "that you may be strengthened in your inner being with power through his Spirit and that Christ may dwell in your hearts through faith, as you are being rooted and grounded in love." He prays further, that "you may have the power to comprehend with all the saints, what is the breadth and length and height and depth, and to know the love of Christ that surpasses knowledge, so that you may be filled with all the fullness of God" (3:16–19).

What interests me about this prayer is the apparent passivity of those prayed for. Paul asks for a number of wondrous things to be done to and for the followers of Christ. God, the Holy Spirit, and Christ are the actors here. We are the receivers of their action. In recollection, one creates the space in which God may act upon the world and us, and a place where Christ may dwell. Recollection allows our shallow roots, vainly seeking to be nourished by material goods and success, to become rooted and grounded in the fertile soil of love.

Recollection, in my experience, is not something you do once and then are finished with. It must be replenished continually. You have to keep taking back holy ground. There is an endless supply of critters eager to move into the space you have created. Erect fences. Drag your foot in a circle around your hearth. Mark your territory. Hire guards. Keep watch, as Jesus admonishes.

Each time I return to the hermitage I marvel anew at the reclaiming I am required to do. Years ago, when I began praying at the hermitage, I did not want to harm any creature. The word soon got out that I was an easy touch and generations of field mice moved in from the whole of Jackson County. I sealed their entrances. I bought ultrasonic pest resisters. I bought humane traps. I caught the little boogers in my hands and hauled them out to the pasture. They came back. They chewed up the bedspread. They nested in the old trunk. They littered the floor. They got into the bird feed. Now I kill them.

I say to them, "You have four hundred acres out here. These two hundred square feet are mine." Snakes, spiders, toads, beetles, even a duck—when your back is turned something will come crawling over the sill. Webs in the privy. Raccoons in the woodpile. Coyotes passing through. Stuff wants to get in, take over if it can. All God's creatures are on the lookout for a little shelter, a place out of the rain and cold. To be filled with all the fullness of God instead of being full of the world's clutter and pain, we have to create and maintain space. We empty ourselves, but the world keeps sneaking back, slipping a hand under the door, oozing in through the cracks. There are mind weasels, mind wasps, mind lizards, and assorted other varmints that will settle in and build a nest at the first opportunity. Pesky attitudes, irritating notions, false assumptions, flit in and out, peck at the windows, skitter across the floor, chew at the baseboard.

When it comes to holy ground and the recollection that is part of creating it, the rule seems to be squatter's rights. Whoever gets there first, lays claim, and stays the longest, gets the space.

BUTTERSCOTCH understood squatter's rights. There was the time when the larger two-legged one brought two kittens home. They moved in next to Butterscotch's cage on the deck and were annoying her. She turned and gave them an unfriendly look out of narrowed eyes; then, fluffing herself out more and tucking in her paws, she returned to her recollection.

Butterscotch was determined not to give up her territorial prerogative to the two intruders. Later, when she entered the kitchen and discovered the kittens playing there, she had to take a big chunk of time out of her recollection to get the kitchen marked again with her scent. She hopped about for thirty minutes rubbing her chin on chair legs, the bottom doors of cupboards, wastebaskets, woodwork, and our feet. Meanwhile the kittens approached and retreated with timid curiosity. When the marking was completed to her satisfaction, she peppered the floor with droppings and then headed for the kittens' bed. Squeezing her ample hips into the small box, she backed into a corner and peed on the kittens' blanket. Finally, assured that the place was hers again, she lay under the table with hind legs stretched out surveying the kitchen like a queen. The kittens, pouncing on her head and attacking from behind, tried to get her to play. She remained detached and recollected on her holy ground.

LOTS OF PEOPLE these days are seeking recollection, writing books about it, urging us to do it. It seems like a nice idea all right—until you try it. What a lot of the books don't tell you about is the terror. To know the love of Christ that surpasses knowledge may mean not knowing much of anything else.

With the peace and quiet of recollection may come the stark edge of fear that this doing nothing, this being, this offering of oneself for God to be the actor, cannot possibly be enough. It all seems so passive. Do something, produce, perform, earn your keep. Don't just sit there. It may be good and well for Mary to offer space in herself for God to dwell and be born into the world, but few of us possess the radical belief such recollection requires.

What matters in recollection and the deeper experience of contemplation is not the doing and accomplishing. What matters is relationship, the being with. We create holy ground and give birth to Christ in our time not by doing but by believing and by loving the mysterious Infinite One who stirs within. This requires trust that something of great and saving importance is growing and kicking its heels in you.

The angel summoned Mary, betrothed to Joseph, from the rather safe place of conventional wisdom to a realm where few of the old rules would make much sense. She entered that unknown called "virgin territory." She was on her own there. No one else could judge for her the validity of her experience.

She can measure her reality against Scripture, the teachings of her tradition, her reason and intellect, and the counsel of wise friends. But finally it is up to her. The redemption of the creation is resting on the consent—the choice of this mortal woman to believe fearlessly that what she is experiencing is true. And to claim and live out that truth by conceiving the fruit of salvation.

To be virgin means to be one, whole in oneself, not perforated by the concerns of the conventional norms and authority, or the powers and principalities. To be virgin, then, is in a sense to be recollected.

Though recollection appears to be passive, it is worth noting that *conceive* is an active verb. Its Latin root means "to seize, to take hold of." Because Mary is recollected, she is able to take hold of God. Elizabeth, in whom John the Baptist leaps for joy at the approach of Christ in Mary, exclaims, "Blessed is she who believed that there would be fulfillment of what was spoken to her from the Lord." Blessed are all virgins, male and female, who believe that there will be fulfillment of what is spoken to them by the angelic messengers of grace.

Jesus observed, "Without me you can do nothing" (John 15:5). Yet we act, for the most part, as though without us God can do nothing. We think we have to make Christmas come, which is to say we think we have to bring about the redemption of the universe on our own. When all God needs is a willing womb, a place of safety, nourishment, and love. "Oh, but nothing will get done," you say. "If I don't do it, Christmas won't happen." And we crowd out Christ with our fretful fears.

God asks us to give away everything of ourselves. The gift of greatest efficacy and power that we can offer God and creation is not our skills, gifts, abilities, and possessions. The wise men had their gold, frankincense, and myrrh. Paul and Peter had their preaching. Mary offered only space, love, belief. What is it that delivers Christ into the world—preaching, art, writing, scholarship, social justice? Those are all gifts well worth sharing. But preachers lose their charisma, scholarship grows pedantic, social justice alone cannot save us. In the end, when all other human gifts have met their inevitable limitation, it is the recollected one, the bold virgin with a heart in love with God who makes a sanctuary of her life who delivers Christ who then delivers us.

Try it. Leave behind your briefcase and notes and proof texts. Leave behind your honed skills and knowledge. Leave the Christmas decorations up in the attic. Go to someone in need and say, "Here, all I have is Christ." And find out that that is enough.

Imagine a Christmas service where the worshipers come in their holiday finery to find a sanctuary empty of all the glittering decorations, silent of holiday carols. What if this year you canceled the church decoration committee and the worship committee and called off the extra choir rehearsals and the church school pageant?

What if on Christmas Eve people came and sat in the dim pews, and someone stood up and said, "Something happened here while we were all out at the malls, while we were baking cookies and fretting about whether we bought our brother-in-law the right gift: *Christ was born. God is here*"? We wouldn't need the glorious choruses and the harp and the bell choir and the organ. We wouldn't need the tree strung with lights. We wouldn't have to deny that painful dissonance between the promise and hope of Christmas and a world wracked with sin and evil. There wouldn't be that embarrassing conflict over the historical truth of the birth stories and whether or not Mary was really a virgin. And no one would have to preach sermons to work up our belief.

All of that would seem gaudy and shallow in comparison to the sanctity of that still sanctuary. And we, hushed and awed by something greater and wiser and kinder than we, would kneel of one accord in the stillness. A peace would settle over the planet like a velvet coverlet drawn over a sleeping child. The world would recollect itself and discover itself held in the womb of the

Mother of God. We would be filled with all the fullness of God, even as we filled the emptiness of the Savior's heart with ours.

The intensity and strain that many of us bring to Christmas must suggest to some onlookers that, on the whole, Christians do not seem to have gotten the point of it. Probably few of us have the faith or the nerve to tamper with hallowed Christmas traditions on a large scale or with our other holiday cele-brations. But a small experiment might prove interesting. What if, instead of *doing* something, we were to *be* something special? Be womb. Be dwelling for God. *Be recollected*, and be surprised.

THE KITTENS WERE charging around the kitchen attempting high jumps over the stool, chasing and attacking each other. Butterscotch roused herself, stretching and yawning. She sat up and washed her face and ears. "Tzimtzum," she murmured in low tones from the back of her throat. In quietness and trust was her strength.

CHAPTER 28

Spring Was Coming: Maybe
Acedia: The Demon of the Noonday Sun

*S*pring was coming, maybe, but it sure wasn't here yet. Chill damp air still cloaked us in a colorless haze, and gray days stretched into monotonous sameness. Butterscotch, the rabbit, kept to herself now. Ahs grew sullen, tearing up newspapers on the back porch and defiantly pulling things out of the wastebaskets and dropping them in the middle of the floor. The gray kitten, Seal, stayed in the garage alone. The other kitten, Teva, was missing, but no one spoke much of her.

Teva was apparently a victim of Pumpkin, the neighbor's tomcat. Pumpkin was used to the dog and the rabbit; they were here before he was and were not his kind. But the kittens were another matter, and he stalked them with jealous zeal. Late one afternoon we heard horrid cat screams. When we rushed outside, we saw Pumpkin leap nimbly from the maple while Teva cowered at the far end of a high limb. We coaxed her down and comforted her, but the next day she disappeared. So we ran an ad:

LOST. BELOVED KITTEN.
Black with white socks and moustache.

But no one had seen such a kitten. We prayed for her at mealtime blessings and, for a while, we called and searched. But then we stopped.

A malaise settled over the household, as I went about muttering to the heavy gray skies, "Now is the winter of our discontent." The two-legged ones snapped at one another, pouted, and pined after imagined lost chances and glamour in distant places. Even the prom issue of *Seventeen* magazine did little to lift the gloom. The beautiful young women on the arms of handsome guys going to far-away places only intensified the hopelessly retarded social scene at the local high school.

Now is the winter of our discontent. The barren landscape and harsh wind strip us of anything false or contrived that will not hold up under the bitter scrutiny of this season which takes us to the basics—food, shelter, warmth, love.

The rabbit was growing weary of these gray cold days. The dog stirred in the straw, yawned, and stretched. All of us were tired of our cages and pens, yet we had little ambition to go anywhere else. Some of us got haircuts, which helped briefly, as did new contact lenses and learning to pluck our eyebrows. Cicelia kept trying to rearrange her room, pushing her bed about and plopping boxes of her things in the middle of my study.

THE NAME the early Christians gave for the dullness that had settled over us is *acedia*. The desert fathers and mothers called this oppressive state of spiritual apathy the demon of the noonday sun. Evagrius warned, "This demon attacks the monk towards the fourth hour and besieges the soul until the eighth hour. He begins by giving the impression that the sun is hardly moving or not moving at all, and the day has at least forty hours."[37] Indifference and boredom replace ardor and passion for the things of God. The miserable soul is sick of both God and self.

The purpose of this dry discontent is seen as part of the final purification of the will so that it may be merged without any reserve in God. Acedia abolishes spiritual gluttony as it strips us of our fascination with glamour, ease, and sensory delights. Since God is spirit and must be worshiped in spirit, a soul's worship of God grows over time to be less founded in the satisfaction and entertainment of the senses and more in the dark knowing called faith. Through the harsh succor of the demon of acedia the soul is weaned from its attachment to sensory gratification to a more mature love.

As we begin the spiritual journey, we relate to the holy as it is revealed through the created order and experienced through our will, intellect, and senses. Yet Jesus and the saints tell us there is more to the spiritual life than meets the eye or satisfies the senses. Just what this might be is hard to describe. Some call it unknowing, the worship of spirit and truth, being born again in the spirit, or, simply, faith. Although it was the miracles that brought out the crowds, Jesus repeatedly said that was not why he had come. And, further, he praised those whose trust in him came not from facts and objective data but from the more obscure and intangible certainty of faith. However it is described, there appears to be a way to be with God that transcends the limitations of ordinary human experience. Yet it is not in itself

142

extraordinary. It does not involve visions, ecstasies, or any kind of spiritual fireworks. It is a more refined, subtle, and deeper being with God.

Acedia relates to care, anxiety, grief. What seems to underlie this unenviable condition is the fear and sadness that maybe spring won't come, that maybe we won't get through this heavy Lent, that the human condition of sin and frailty is not going to be overcome by a new prom dress.

SPRING IS COMING, maybe. A man whom much of the world will declare is God is making his way inexorably into death. He is going to do that ordinary thing people do everyday: he is going to suffer and die. What makes this different is that it is God who is doing it and that God overcomes the sting of it all by being God, by being the One who attains victory not by escaping evil or by beating it to a pulp but by surrendering to it and going right through the heart of it while remaining God.

As we watch Jesus walking toward the cross, we want to call out: "Don't do it. Don't go that way. And for heaven's sake, don't ask us to do it, too." But he, who has set his face like flint, will not hide from the insult and spitting. No, the amazing claim is that this gray day, this aging body, this meager life houses glory. And our reluctant following after Jesus is grounded in the slim hope that somehow, some way, this is true.

Spring doesn't come from some far distant place like an eagerly awaited guest bringing exotic presents. Spring recoils, bounces up from the heart of winter, and jiggles before us like a jack-in-the-box. The joke is on us. We strain to turn the crank that sets free joy, and just when our guard is down and we think life is only a meaningless turning to an idiotic tune, out pops Jesus winking his eye. "Now, die!" he says. We, who thought we were chasing joy and were hot on its trail, find ourselves swallowed up by life and dwelling in the inner parts of the God who creates joy.

"The function of acedia is to cure the soul of its innate tendency to seek and rest in spiritual joys; to confuse Reality with the joy given by the contemplation of Reality," writes Evelyn Underhill.[38] The demon of the midday sun shows up to accompany us through Lent to help us discover the difference between joy and the Source from which it springs.

A PATIENT in a mental hospital once came up, fixed me with a piercing gaze, and hissed, "God is a consuming fire. The Lord, thy God, is a jealous God." If ever I felt I had received a word from the Lord, I did that day. I didn't much like it either. Being reminded of God's jealous nature may make us uncomfortable. God's jealousy is disturbing in part because it suggests that

God is vulnerable, somehow in need of us, and subject to a passionate desire for our fidelity. For us, jealousy and envy are upsetting, embarrassing emotions. God has commanded us not to covet. So how is it that God gets by with it? Perhaps it is because we matter. We are creatures God Almighty wants to be with. God is drawn to us in love. Our discomfort with the biblical truth of God's jealous love may have more to do with our low opinion of ourselves than a personality failure on God's part. A jealous God is a God who is not content to see us settle for anything less than the holiness for which we have been created.

Amazingly, God wants to be with us and has gone to great lengths to get our attention—and that is almost more than we can bear. What do we know about being company for God? For thousands of years we have been trying to get it right.

Someone hears a word from the Lord and says: "Here, do it like this. Here are the answers we are seeking." We give names to Truth. We compose prayers and rituals. We sew up little suits for Truth to wear. But over time, Truth grows beyond the suits. Its legs stretch below the cuffs, and shirt sleeves ride up to the elbows. We try to stuff Truth back in its tearing clothes. We sew patches here and there. We get into fights about the right color of patches. We pay more attention to the clothes than to Truth.

Truth condescends to wear the forms we give it only briefly. Jesus bursts the wineskin of the tomb we called death. The Church shudders, draws in its breath, and exhales, bursting its seams. Some panic. Some become weary and simply turn away. When Truth, as we have known and cherished it, begins to grow beyond the forms that have mediated it for us—that is, language, institutions, rituals—dread acedia may set in.

For a good part of the journey our relationship with the holy is largely self-serving. We seek God for our benefit. Then, during this tedious Lent, we go seeking help and find a forlorn God carrying a cross.

Jesus asks, "How long have I been with you, and you still do not understand? I want to be with you—not just to bring you peace, joy, and good, but even more because I need a place to lay my head. Will you stay with me one hour?" Constrained by sanctity, God cannot come too close to mortals. So God paces outside, blowing into his palms, stomping his feet to keep warm, while we pray for things to be better and better and better in the long winter of our discontent.

We usually begin our acquaintance with God from the outside in. Jesus is external, beyond us. I learn about God from the historical record, the witness of the Church, Scripture—through forms, rituals, disciplines, words, symbols. Could it not also be possible to know God from the inside out? To experience God from God's interior reality, a reality which the forms seek to represent or express? "Where are you staying?" John's two disciples ask Jesus. "Come and see," he says. And they go and see where he lives, and remain there with him that day (John 1:38-39). How would it be for you to live in the place where Christ lives? To eat and sleep and move about in his home?

In Jesus Christ God is inviting us to see things from the inside out, to stay where God stays, to indwell divine reality and truth. God requires a clean heart and a right spirit. Our attachment to the sensationalism of our times creates the urgency and fear that fuel spiritual unchastity.

The shift from knowing Jesus from the outside in to the inside out may be perilous. The structures of meaning, categories for naming and holding one's experience and truth, begin to disintegrate. They no longer work to contain one's experience of self and Christ. We may feel confused. What was certain and absolute seems less so. We may feel abandoned by the God of our past experience. We may think we are losing our faith.

In an act of reckless courage Meister Eckhart prayed: "God! Rid Me of God!"[39] God is beyond meaning, beyond any categories and names we might apply to God and our experience of God. Eckhart recognized the temptation to become attached to the forms and names we give the Ineffable Unnameable One.

JOHN OF THE CROSS tells of a person who for more than ten years profited by a cross roughly made out of a blessed palm and held together by a pin twisted around it. "He carried it about and never would part with it until I took it from him and he was not a person of poor judgment or little intelligence." I imagine the little saint yanking the cherished cross out of the hands of this startled soul. John identifies such practices as spiritual avarice and lust. What he is condemning here is possessiveness of heart and attachment to the objects or practices. "For such attachment is contrary to poverty of spirit which is intent only upon the substance of the devotion, since true devotion comes from the heart and looks only to the truth and substance represented by spiritual objects."[40]

Acedia is that pain of withdrawal we feel as God is yanking our cherished means of knowing divine reality away from us. Our spiritual sense is still too unrefined and accustomed to spiritual glitz to appreciate the subtler flavor of pure faith. Hence we feel the aridity and dullness.

As God calls us away from familiar ways of knowing God, what is left? Nothing but loss and a cross on a hill with a dead man hanging from it?

Stay there a bit longer. Wait. Be confused. Consent to not knowing or understanding. Something you cannot even conceive of is preparing to spring up. Something so new, so radically different that your mind cannot name it, is sending out roots in the silent darkness. Tiny roots are thrusting through the heavy earth, threading their way around stones to living water. Wait some more. Oh, it's hard to bear the ambiguity. We want to plow up the soil and rip out the root, to hold it to the light, dissect it, name its parts, and feel that secure sense of power and control where we can say this is this and that is that.

Yet we can wait. We can trust until it stands before us in the morning sun. Then we reach in joy to touch once more our beloved.

"Don't cling to me," it says (John 20:17).

God wants to be with us, desires our devotion, and is jealous when we choose to be with anything other than God. Are we ready to know reality itself rather than the gifts it gives us—to know and love the giver more than the gift?

Here is a spare, bare love. All that is left is a man walking alone carrying what will kill him, the merciless weight of mortality. Here is only a naked soul surrendered to God, slung from the pillar of its own predicament. If God could enter into our humanity with humble love, can it be too much for us to do the same? There is no other way into the kingdom. Here, this is what is so: we all screw up. We all are limited and frail. And we can rejoice because we do not have to lie about it anymore.

THE WIND RATTLES the few dead leaves still hanging onto the pear tree. Pumpkin skulks down the alley. Seal mopes about missing her playmate. Diana lights a candle at evening prayer. "I really believe Teva is all right, Mom," she tells me.

Spring tenses in the roots of the pear tree. And all the cats and mortals who were ever carried off in the teeth of jealousy or simply in the way of things, all innocence defiled, all vulnerability exploited, sink with a sigh into a white dawn that stretches like a shroud wound round the world. "Come follow me," the Dawn whispers. And we are all invited to take another step into that place beyond knowing, beyond feeling, where everything really is all right.

CHAPTER 29

Learning a New Skill
Giving Jesus Away

*S*pring brought two owls into the neighborhood. They called all day and night in a repertoire of low throaty calls, clucks, and whistles. At dusk they really revved up, hooting until the trees resounded; then they were silent for a while. One day a young owl appeared, and we watched it hop and wobble across the street and up to the shrubs of the neighbor's house. Later we saw it perched on the rocker on the front porch, its parent calling from a nearby tree trying in vain to teach it the difference between tree branches and rocking chairs. In spite of dive bomb attacks by teams of blue jays, the three seem to have settled in.

And this spring Butterscotch learned to purr. She began shortly after Seal gave birth to her kittens in the cardboard box at the bottom of the cellar stair beneath the rabbit's cage; the kittens, probably sired by Pumpkin, made a young mom of Seal, barely a year old. Up until the kittens arrived, Butterscotch had been mostly silent, except for a low gurgling coo in the back of her throat when we held her close. But after the kittens came and Seal spent most of her time curled in the box nursing and cleaning her children, Butterscotch's coo grew into low steady clucks.

I have heard that rabbits coo when they are in heat. Perhaps the drama of birth going on directly below had put the notion in Butterscotch's head to be a mother herself. Or maybe she just wanted to learn a new skill this summer.

The new kittens mewed. The jays screamed. The squirrels chattered and scolded. The dog barked. The owls hooted. Why wouldn't a rabbit want to purr?

"I HAVE NO SILVER OR GOLD," bold Peter tells the lame man in Acts. "But look at me. I give you what I have. Walk in Jesus' name" (3:6). What passed from

Peter to the lame man that unbound his legs? What passes among us that brings healing hope and peace? Peter said its name was Jesus.

I've been wondering what it means to give someone Jesus. What does it mean to have Jesus to give away? When the transaction is accomplished, the result is unmistakable: healing, freedom, and a fellow kicking up his heels.

The lame man sees Peter and John going up to the Temple and asks for alms. The two look down intently at the man, and Peter says, "Look at us." The man fixes his attention on them expectantly.

Is this how it is done, by looking at one another? What is it like for someone in possession of privilege, abundance, and grace to ask to be looked at by one in need? Many of us would shrink from such looking. We turn away from the victim of catastrophic illness, the homeless woman on the street, the survivor of a devastating flood or famine.

Don't stare at me. Don't convict me of my complicity in your losses. Don't make me think about how you are my brother. If you look at me, you might see my guilt and sin. So let's avert our eyes while I drop a few coins in your hat. I will not look too intently at you and certainly will not meet your eyes with mine. For then I would have to see that at any moment we could change places. Don't remind me of the frailty of my flesh. Don't make me see that one day my legs may no longer carry me and I, too, will depend upon the generosity of strangers.

For some moments the three gaze at each other. Two are looking down; the man on the ground is looking up. Did it feel like further humiliation for him to have to look and be looked at in order to receive a bit of charity? Was he ashamed to expose his withered body to their eyes?

WE ARE APT either to despise the weak and needy or to pity them. We prefer to attribute their losses to their personal failures. He was careless. She should have gone to the doctor sooner. Surely no grim twist of fate could have caused this one's pain. For then I, too, would be vulnerable to something out of my control. An act of God or humanity that would leave me lying on a curb begging for help could broadside me. Better to believe this is somehow this man's fault.

On the other hand, we may feel overwhelmed by the other's need. I turn away saying I already have more than I can handle. There is nothing I can do that would make any real difference anyway. Helping you will diminish me.

Then Peter says it: "I have no silver or gold. But what I have I give you, in the name of Jesus Christ of Nazareth, stand up and walk." We'd rather give silver or gold, tangible, material things. Let's put this Jesus stuff in a bottle and hand out tracts about the Eight Spiritual Laws. Here I have no silver or gold, but listen to my sermon, buy my book, swallow these vitamins.

I cannot give what I do not have. I cannot give another faith, truth, peace, love, and forgiveness if those things are not in me. If all I possess is silver or gold, if all I possess are ideas and opinions, solutions and advice—then that is all that I will have to give away.

What ought to be unique about a Christian is that he or she has Jesus to give. What is given does not come from us and, therefore, giving it cannot diminish us. The gift only makes its home in us like a treasure in a clay jar. When I feel depleted by responding to the needs of others, I may be trying to give them something other than Jesus.

Peter tells the astounded crowd that it is not his and John's devotion or power that makes the man stand up. It is not their love or skill or anything about them. It is faith in the name of Jesus, faith, that is, through Jesus that raises the man to his feet. Peter and John had simply given the man their *faith*—their conviction of God's saving activity in Jesus the Nazarene. They gave the man the power inherent in their belief in the identity of Jesus Christ. Through Jesus they had access to God Almighty and freedom to direct that power to those in need. This is the treasure, and it is powerful enough to restore life to withered limbs.

Henri Nouwen tells of a time he spent at the Trappist monastery in Genesee, New York. He was weary and felt pressed by the burdens of teaching. When a group of students came to the monastery and asked him to lead them in a retreat, he was distressed and overwhelmed by yet another request at the place where he had hoped to escape demands. He went to the abbot to explain why he could not take on this group. To his dismay the abbot told him he was going to do it. Nouwen protested, "Why should I spend my sabbatical preparing all those things?"

"Prepare?" the abbot replied. "You've been a Christian for forty years and a priest for twenty, and a few high school students want to have a retreat. Why do you have to prepare? What those boys and girls want are to be a part of your life in God for a few days. If you pray half an hour in the morning, sing in the choir for an hour, and do your spiritual reading, you will have so much to say you could give ten retreats."[41]

Peter does not give the man at the Temple information or counsel or even lay his hands on him. What does the man hear in those words as he takes Peter's hand and feels himself rising to his feet? What does the man see in Peter's eyes? Is it not a glimpse of Peter's life in God?

Evelyn Underhill writes: "It is wonderfully impressive to see a soul that really loves God, and really feels awe and delight, speaking to God." She recalls what William Penn said of George Fox: "The most awful, living, reverent frame I ever felt or beheld, was his in prayer."[42]

Perhaps you have been in the hallowed presence of someone who was so surrendered to God, who had so transcended the rote, mechanical quality of shallow prayer, that the one praying became a means of revelation. Just as Moses' shining face was testimony to the glory of divine and human communion, beholding a free soul at prayer is inspiring. "My goodness," we think, "he is really serious about this!" Our doubt is exposed and converted by the faith of this soul's prayer, which then awakens our soul's prayer, and carries us all a little deeper into the reality of God.

It can be enough to make a lame man walk.

THE WORLD HAS a voracious hunger for scandal, the intimate details, especially the perceived sins of those in leadership. And all of us, including Peter, have plenty to hide. His faith was hardly a model of purity and steadfastness. But something happened to him at this point on his journey. From beholding Jesus as the Christ in a boat swarming with fish, to a hasty promise of his fidelity, to the rooster's crow, he had his nose rubbed in the truth of his sin and faithlessness.

Ministry requires us to be willing to be looked at, to be seen as our true selves, even to ask those we serve to look closely at us. Many of us shrink from such scrutiny. Those we look up to and those we allow to gaze down at us in our brokenness need to be people who are willing to be seen. They need not be without sin, but they do need to be able to be naked and not be ashamed.

Peter could have stayed stuck back in the boat groveling in all those fish, protesting that he was a sinful man. He could still be sitting in the courtyard weeping over his betrayal of Jesus. He could be so ashamed and wracked with guilt that he never ventured into the world with the treasure Christ had entrusted to him. But something happened to him between the awareness of his sin and guilt and that afternoon at the Beautiful Gate. Something pulled away the hand that shame had placed upon his lips and set him free to give to another in need a relationship in God so palpable and powerful it could make a lame man dance.

Try it. Say to the world begging on the threshold of the Temple, "Look at me. Really look at me. I have no silver or gold. I have nothing to give you to ease your pain or bring you joy. God is more powerful and effective in my life than I am. I have nothing, am nothing, except for this life I have in Christ. You and I are one. If your legs are paralyzed, then so are mine. If my heart is full of grace, then so is yours. Here, take this faith of mine. If you had your own, you wouldn't be asking for help."

This leaning confidently into the power of God moment by moment with vulnerability and honesty, this willingness to be seen and to know forgiveness through Jesus, is to return to the garden and to be naked and unashamed.

Isn't this what lifts you up in the end? The gaze of another who doesn't hurry on past but who looks you full in the face, seeing you just as you are without pity or judgment. It is a wonderful thing to be seen in this way. It is a healing thing to be seen and appreciated for who you really are, in your need as well as in your dignity and holiness. Such seeing and being seen is no less than the love of God made known in Christ Jesus.

In Jesus, God came to look upon us in our need with compassion. In Jesus we look God in the face. In that looking we are forgiven, accepted, loved.

AT TIMES THE CHURCH has attempted to give Jesus to the world in ways that have patronized or insulted the receivers. We have shoved Jesus down people's throats with threats of damnation. We have bored people to death with unimaginative, rigid doctrine. We have betrayed the trust of people with hypocritical leaders. The challenge for the Church today is to discover ways to give Jesus instead of silver and gold. The Church needs to offer the world its life in God, instead of glitz and glitter. To do that the Church must discover and nurture its life in God. This requires it to be willing to have nothing else—to be deliberately poor or at least able to let go. It has to be willing to look the unbeliever in the eye as a brother or sister and to discover the power that resides not in its wealth of programs, theology, art, music, or marketing savvy but in its poverty and total dependence on God.

A preacher looks out at the rows of worshipers seeking meaning and healing in their lives. Maybe all they hope for are a few coins, enough to get them through the week. With love, the preacher sees their immense need. Are there clergy bold as Peter who will say, "Look at me. I have nothing for you—no easy answers, quick fixes, miracle cures. All I have is this faith I have in Jesus"?

Then what do you suppose happens? How do we know when Jesus has been passed among us?

Maybe we can put it this way: *we get back up on our feet again*. The treasure we pass among us is personal worth, freedom, and independence. God does not give us silver and gold, things that only increase our dependence on the source of the silver and gold. The gift of Christ is the internal empowerment to give birth to our own life in God, to bring about fully whom God has made us to be.

ONE SUMMER I asked our daughters to practice an old skill and learn a new one. Cicelia decided she would learn to dive off the high diving board. Diana learned to play the guitar so she could entertain us with the music of her favorite rock star. The baby owl learned to hoot. Me? Well, I wanted to learn to make the lame walk.

CHAPTER 30

Christianity and the Occult
Ahs Gets His Fortune Told

*A*hs had been hankering to have his fortune told for a while. The notion took hold in moments of anxiety. The dog actually knew little about Tarot cards and the occult arts. Molly, the spaniel down the alley, claimed she had been to a psychic a time or two. The new Dalmatian two doors away boasted she had had her astrological chart done; she told that notations were made concerning her diet, best times for breeding, flea protection, and kennel maintenance.

Ahs didn't have anything specific that he wanted to know about improving the quality of his life. He ate Best Buy Old Roy dog food. Since that long ago visit to the vet, he didn't think much about breeding. His pen was cleaned fairly routinely. And as for flea protection, he scratched. Rather, he was looking for some general assurance that things would turn out all right, and, yes, to be honest, that one day he'd get to catch a cat.

His interest in the occult had come on shortly after Butterscotch, the golden Rex rabbit, was killed. The sudden death of the wise and beloved pet was a painful shock to the household. Ever since old Sarah, the yellow hound, had died, Ahs and Butterscotch had been companions. They spent many afternoons stretched out under the pear tree, Butterscotch in her pen, Ahs tethered to the porch. There they discussed theology, current events, and the foibles of the two-leggeds they watched over. In recent months they forged a deeper alliance over their mutual dislike of the household's recent additions, two uppity cats.

Now the rabbit's pen stood empty on the deck. Ahs couldn't quite say what she meant to him. He felt calmer, more at home and comfortable with himself around her. He found it hard to think of Butterscotch and her death. His mind would rest lightly on her absence and then skip quickly to some other thought before it slid into the dark painful place of the truth that she was gone.

It was while he was casting about for something else to think of that the Ouijia board eased into his mind. Molly found it in the trash and dragged it over one day. There was some sticky sweet stuff on it the two licked off. Bits of caramel popcorn, something else—maybe ice cream—and the entire board smelled wonderfully of pizza. Snuffling and licking, they gave it a thorough going over, but neither turned up any pepperoni.

That evening the two sat before it under the moon. They pushed the funny shaped piece of wood around with their paws the way they had watched the teenagers do. "Butterscotch are you there?" Molly yipped. But since they couldn't read, let alone spell, they soon gave up and started knocking the little piece of wood back and forth, tossing it in the air, and playing catch until it was a slimy, chewed-up wad. The next day one of the owls snatched it up and packed it into a loose section of his nest.

After Molly went home, Ahs had a disturbing dream about an irate rabbit chasing him and biting his heels. "You stinky dog, leave me alone! Don't go poking your snout where you have no business!" The rabbit hissed at him like a cat. Ahs ran, panting until his lungs ached, as the rabbit loomed larger and larger and more ferocious behind him. In desperation he climbed a tree, toenails scraping and clawing the bark. Clinging precariously to a branch, he looked down to see a cat with long ears barking at him from the ground. He awoke exhausted and stayed in his pen most of the day.

Children deprived of love turn to magic, observes novelist Barbara Kingsolver. Grief and fear of further loss had left the dog vulnerable to magic. And underneath the sadness and sense that life was not as certain and predictable as he had thought was the fact that he felt ashamed at how things seemed to be turning out. He just wanted some peace of mind, the peace of personal power, of knowing what was ahead. So when one of the neighborhood owls announced that for the price of a bone, he could tell their futures by reading hairballs and counting ticks, Ahs's ears perked up.

Of course, the cats wanted to come along, too. Seal's kitten had taken to bragging around the neighborhood that he channeled Puss in Boots, Aslan, and he felt he was just getting a bead on Cleopatra's kitty. Ahs wasn't much impressed with metaphysics or the supernatural. He'd just got to feeling so anxious and lonely lately that he thought this might calm him down.

DIANA BROUGHT HOME a book on witchcraft from the library the other day, and the book of spells stimulated an important discussion in our household.

In the intense world of an adolescent, full of yearning and passion yet possessing minimal power to satisfy those insistent desires, one can see how such a book might have appeal. My daughters told me they know kids who are into witchcraft and who play with Ouija boards. I advised the girls that things like this could be dangerous. "Mom, I don't get it. What's wrong with this? They are only fooling around."

How does one explain the ancient biblical prohibition against the occult in a way a teenager can accept? I made a stab, "God has gone to a whole lot of trouble to help us by sending us Jesus, who shows us the way and the truth for our lives. It hurts God when we ignore that way and try to gain supernatural knowledge by some other means."

Amazingly, Cecilia understood. "Yeah, Mom," she observed thoughtfully. "It's like if you spent a long time making an apple pie and whoever you made it for turns up their nose and says, they'd rather have glue."

Her older sister continued, "Yes, but Mom, Jesus doesn't tell you very much and you just have to wait and see how things turn out. And besides, I don't mean to be rude or anything, but he can be kind of boring."

"Remember when you were baptized and confirmed, you made promises to God to be faithful to Jesus and always belong to him? To turn away or give up on him when things are hard is like breaking an important promise to a friend or committing adultery in a marriage. If we can stick with Jesus long enough, even when things aren't going our way and we feel like he is nowhere around, we will eventually find out he can give us all we need and more. We may even discover that it is not he who is boring, but that we are the boring ones."

"Whatever," shrugged my fifteen-year-old, reminding me to save my sermons for the pulpit.

OCCULT MEANS literally "to cover up, conceal, shut off from view." Occultism relates to matters involving the action or influence of supernatural or supernormal powers. It encompasses a wide range of theories and practices involving a belief in and knowledge or use of supernatural forces or beings.

Contemporary popular spirituality is a minefield to which the modern Church, as a whole, has done little to provide a map for safe passage or a means to identify what might go off in one's face and what is harmless. For some, occult is considered synonymous with spirituality. Large sections of bookstores, book clubs, and catalogs are devoted to the occult. The boundary between Christian spirituality and occultism is increasingly blurred in our time. Many persons see nothing harmful in such practices as divination, channeling, and astrology. The occult often comes beautifully packaged with angels, spirit guides, happy thoughts, and holy sentiments. It is not unusual for the occult to claim as its masters certain mystics and saints of Christian spirituality, notes Evelyn Underhill. Spirituality, once confined to religion, now shows up in health care, business, and sports. The modern seeker, who often is not biblically or theologically literate, may be bewildered and misled by the confusing mix.

Just because something is called spiritual doesn't make it good; not all spirituality is benevolent spirituality. Some of it is perverted, feeble, and arrogant. Not everything in the supernatural world is equally wholesome. The realm of the spirit contains evil as well as good. Paul takes pains to remind us of "the spiritual forces of evil in the heavenly places" (Eph. 6:12).

The natural world has necessary limits and boundaries beyond which we go at great risk to our bodies. If I jump off a building, I will not sprout wings and fly but will crush myself on the unyielding earth. There are also limits in the spiritual realm, and to ignore such limits is to risk the health of one's soul. Religion provides the boundaries and guidelines for entering the spiritual realm with protection. Part of the purpose of Jesus is to provide safe passage through the murky, confusing spirit realm to union with God.

Spirituality has its seasons, and there is a time for adolescence in the life in the spirit, just as in our psychological and physiological development. Puberty of the spirit brings exuberance and excesses. Teenage spirituality, which can appear in us at any age, seeks out intensity; it is egocentric and impressionable and takes risks. Headstrong, it thinks it knows it all, resists advice, and expects to live forever. Teenage spirituality rebels against the limits and boundaries that religion furnishes as it is driven to discover for itself why such limits exist.

In Acts, we read that Paul met up with a young girl who had psychic gifts. The slave girl with a spirit of divination brought in a lot of money for her owners with her fortune-telling. She followed Paul around for days yelling, "These men are slaves of the most high God, who proclaim to you a way of salvation." Finally Paul, annoyed, turned and addressed the spirit in the girl: "I order you in the name of Jesus Christ to come out of her." Luke tells us it came out that very hour.

Like the slave girl, some people possess such abilities or develop them through prayer and deepening sensitivity to God. The tradition in spiritual guidance is unanimous about the appropriate response to such phenomena: ignore them. As fascinating, frightening, and exhilarating as they may be, they are only distractions. One can find variations of the story, in Christian as well as other religious traditions, about the disciple who tells the master, "When I pray I see the heavens opened, full of angels coming and going. I see Jesus seated on the throne, and I hear the heavenly choruses!" "Hmm, that's too bad. I am very sorry," observes the master, shaking his head, "but I suspect if you ignore it, it will go away."

Extraordinary spiritual experiences, sensations, and visions are suspect and likely say more about the needs of the one who receives them than about anything else. The experience of psychic phenomena, special powers and abilities, and somehow transcending ordinary reality are seen by saints and teachers as periods of spiritual growth to respect, learn from, pass through, but not get stuck in. Yet such shenanigans do sell, as bookstores, psychic hotlines, and the unnamed girl who hounded Paul attest.

The caution about getting stuck in the occult is twofold: it can be dangerous and it offends God. The occult compromises our purity and contaminates our soul. It is, as St. John of the Cross notes, *illicit*, leading away from truth to confusion, illusion, illness, and lies. It offends God, who wants to be in loving relationship with us; it leads away from Christ by implicitly denying the efficacy and sufficiency of the work and resurrection of Jesus Christ.

The occult wants to know and to possess rather than to love. Mature spirituality does not find its assurance and peace in one's ability to predict and be prepared for whatever happens, or to control or change events through the strength of one's will and the manipulation of others. Rather, the Christian finds peace in relationship with Jesus, not in the events and circumstances of life. Jesus says, "Do not put your hope and trust in yourself and the things of this world. All of that will eventually fail you. There is another way to live. Surrender in joy and trust to my presence in every moment. The grace, which is sufficient for your every need, is more immediate than your breath. My yoke is easy. And my burden is light."

THE FEATHERED ONES and four-leggeds gathered eagerly for the reading last night under the elm. Afterwards, Ahs felt rather let down. "You will live a long life. You are loved." As for catching a cat, Owl said the ticks were ambiguous. Another reading would be needed. And the price for that would be two bones—with more meat on them this time.

CHAPTER 31

Mudbabes and Humility
From Ashes to Ashes

I said in my heart with regards to human beings that God is testing them to show that they are but animals and the fate of animals is the same; as one dies, so dies the other. They all have the same breath, and humans have no advantage over the animals; for all is vanity. All go to one place; all are from the dust, and all turn to dust again.
—ECCLESIASTES 3:18-20

*S*pring was on the way, and Ahs was feeling sorry for himself. "I am just pitiful," whined the dog. "Pitiful is what it is. My pen is pitiful. My food is pitiful. My body is pitiful. My life is pitiful."

Isabella Hephzibah and Captain Midnight, the two new rabbits, were excited and were itching to scratch their toes in the dirt. They had their eyes on the soft earth with the leaf mold under the hedge south of the house. They would soon rake back the leaves, scrape out a nice trough to stretch out in, and flop over in the moist dirt on their backs.

Captain Midnight also kept stealing glances at Isabella's firm round haunches. Her beauty was renown. Her thick brown-and-white coat glistened in the sun. Her long whiskers swept to the ground. Dark lashes framed her soft brown eyes. When the wild rabbits of the neighborhood first saw her, they put out the word that a queen was among them, for they had never beheld one of their own kind so grand. Surely one as magnificent as she must possess great power and wisdom. They gathered evenings in a reverent circle near her cage and brought her gifts—carrot tops, rose hips, a little alfalfa from their country cousins.

The cats brought offerings too, not to Isabella but to the two-leggeds. Trophies appeared on the threshold—a bird, a mouse, a squirrel tail. I opened the door at dawn to greet the day and was met by some dead thing. "I take no delight in your offerings! Even though you offer me your fatted animals, I will not look upon them. A humble and contrite heart will be quite enough," I muttered, picking up the mouse at arm's length.

Apparently the need to make an offering extends beyond the human species. Something impels us to take a thing we value and are proud of, haul it over to some altar, and lay it out. I wonder if our acts of virtue, service, and sacrifice appear as poignantly off the mark to God as the cats' expressions of devotion littering the back porch appear to me.

What does the Lord require? Acts of justice, a love of kindness, and a humble walk with God, according to Amos. The requirements of justice and love do not seem to be as difficult to offer God as humility. And humility is allusive; once you think you have got it, you've lost it.

Humility comes from the word *humus*. Humus, which is what Isabella is itching to stretch out in, refers to the brown or black material resulting from decomposition of plant or animal matter and forming the organic portion of the soil. The virtue of humility and the earth are intrinsically connected.

A lot about being Christian has to do with coming down where we ought to be and staying there. Here four-legged critters might have an advantage. Spiritual activities like prayer may inflate our egos. Any significant brush with the holy can leave us reeling and unsteady with a tendency for grandiosity and fanaticism. This is why the more one prays, the more one needs to go around barefoot, sit down, lie down, stretch down upon the earth, and stay in close touch with brothers and sisters who crawl, gallop, trot, and slither.

Saint John of the Cross compared contemplation to a ladder. Through prayer the soul ascends the ladder to know and possess the goods and treasures of heaven. But, John noted, the steps of the ladder of prayer are used both for ascent and for descent. Prayer both lifts a soul in God and humiliates that soul in itself.

"Communications, which are truly from God, have this trait: they simultaneously exalt and humble the soul," advises John.[43] This is partly why the spiritual journey is characterized for a long time by so many ups and downs. Loss and frustration follow success. Torment is followed by goodness. The soul finds satisfaction and consolation and tastes a portion of its glory in God, only to find itself slipping into smug superiority. The soul plunges into its humility and tastes a portion of its wretchedness, only to fall into self-effacing debasement. To stand upright before God holding simultaneously the truths of God's holiness, our sin, and our call to be the righteousness of God is a difficult and tenuous balance.

To be humble is not to make comparisons, observed Dag Hammarskjöld: "To have humility is to experience reality, not in relation to ourselves, but in its sacred independence. It is to see, judge, and act from the point of rest in ourselves."[44]

Walking upright on the earth puts considerable distance between the ground and our heads. At the outset, the season of Lent makes our humanity clear—*from ashes to ashes*. The bottom line is that we are going to die and become dust. And just so we won't forget, we wear a smudge of ashes on our brows.

To be human is to encounter limits and to suffer. Through our suffering we have the opportunity to greet and love the sacred vulnerability that resides in the heart of matter and to forgive ourselves for being human. The dying God, all bloody, hanging on a tree, may repulse, offend, or scandalize us—or leave us unmoved and detached. Our response may mirror our inner relationship to our own human frailty. How much compassion and generosity can you bring to yourself in your situation? Not denial, resentment, or blame—just gentle acceptance of who you are in your sacred independence and trust that you have been created and loved by God and are therefore worthy of your own affection and regard.

What is pitiful is when we get the notion we ought not to be pitiful and then take an attitude of contempt toward ourselves. The fact is we are pitiful. All of us, poor and meager, sinners one and all. Can we lower ourselves enough to enter our pitiful reality, live there, and love it with Jesus?

Sometimes I do not know what prayer is beyond the long worn rag of human longing waved toward the heavens like a tattered flag. Today I think prayer has to do with putting down one foot after the other upon this earth, while being honest with ourselves and God about our limitations, and with stretching out in the dirt.

FALL RAINS and a wet winter turned the road to the hermitage into mush. Tractors hauling feed to the cattle tore deep ruts in the lane. Getting to holy ground got harder. Short of a helicopter drop off, to get there I had to go through the mud. The sticky clay stuff sucked at my boots and clung to the soles and dried hard as rock. The ground by the sign announcing Holy Ground, where the cattle like to come to scratch their backs, was pocked with hoof holes.

The name Adam in the creation story in Genesis derives from *adamah*, which means "the ground." It refers to God's forming humanity from the earth. A friend translates Adam as "mudbabe,"and I think "mudbabe" says it nicely.

You don't like the way you are, the way things are? You see room for improvement, need for change? One of the lessons of Lent and Easter is that transformation, healing, and new life come not from a magical *deus ex machina* that drops out of the sky to change whatever it is that doesn't suit us. Rather, as Jesus turns his face to Jerusalem, he invites us to rub our noses in the mud and honestly face the painful realities of our lives and world, as he does the same on the cross.

Feeling a little pitiful yourself? That is why the Almighty came down to earth and let us treat holiness as we treat one another. God comes to teach us to show mercy to one another. God says in Jesus, "Look, my mudbabes, I am not above being human. You ought not to be either. You are going to fail and hurt one another. You are going to make mistakes and come to the limits of your existence, the limits of your flesh, your mind, your faith."

WE ARE FEELING pitiful over our house, which is tipping over. It lists to the north. Drought, rain, freeze, and thaw lift and plow the Kansas soil in waves. The house rides the prairie swells like a great ship—the Queen Mary, I call it—a large hulking house with a peaked roof like a prow. Doors don't shut properly. Marbles roll to the north across the dining room floor. Wallpapering is a nightmare. We hang a picture over a crack and hope the place doesn't fall over before we get our daughters raised and our ship comes in so we can buy a new house.

We had a contractor come to look it over and tell us how much it would cost to repair and strengthen the foundation. After poking about the cellar for a while and taking a slow stroll around the perimeter of the house, he asked cheerily, "Why don't you have your husband buy you a new house?" Then he made the consoling observation that if we ever had an earthquake, an old garage up the street would likely be the first structure in town to crumble. "Your house would be the second to go," he confided confidently.

Well *this* is pitiful. And the foolish ones who purchased such a home are pitiful. But, taking our cue from Christ, we decided the place is worth saving. So the man will be back with his crew and steel beams to perform an operation called, of all things, mud-jacking. They will hoist the house and straighten up our Queen Mary to sail the prairie for a few more years.

But I was embarrassed. How could this have happened? How could we have purchased a home fourteen years ago that was falling over? How could we be so stupid? Other people's houses aren't tipping north. Other people would have had the foundation checked out . . . Other people . . .

I hope your house is soundly upright, but there is a good chance some area in your life is at half tilt. So here's the word of the Lord for today: *Everybody is pitiful. Ashes, ashes we all fall down.* And it is all right, because God's grace is sufficient.

One day all the houses on this earth will have fallen over and crumbled to dust and us with them. Where did we ever get the silly notion we ought not to have a house that leans? Or we ought not to have a body that gets ill, or a life with mistakes and failures, or that it is a shameful, pitiful thing to be a human being and live in a world of human beings?

Go find a place outdoors where there is no concrete smothering the ground. Take off your shoes. Put one bare foot down upon the earth and then the other. Do that a few times. Then kneel down on all fours and press your forehead into the ground. Feel the self-importance, pretense, and the absurd seriousness with which we take ourselves drain off. Smell the earth. Take a good look at the dust from which you came and to which you will return.

Then go have a sandwich and give thanks that you are human and just exactly who you are. Savor and honor the piece of humanity you represent. And taste the goodness of humility.

CHAPTER 32

A Spirit of Harlotry
The God We Worship
vs. the God We Serve

*I*f Cicelia had not stayed in bed until noon, the whole horrible thing probably would not have happened. But school was out and she had taken to sleeping late. Now desecration lay on the threshold and wickedness was strewn across the deck. In its wake the shame-faced animals were slinking about with their tails between their legs.

The day dawned with the herald of birdsong and light glinting off the leaves of the pear tree like tiny mirrors. The animals could hear people stirring in the kitchen. The male two-legged walked briskly out to the garage with his briefcase. Someone started the washing machine. From the dryer vent they caught the moist warm air and scent of softener. But by the time the sun had climbed high in the sky, no breakfast had appeared in their dishes.

Seal tried flinging herself against the screen door where she hung by her claws, spread-eagled, peering into the kitchen. Her efforts failed to rouse anyone. So her son Gavin climbed the cedar tree, leaped to the roof, and trotted over to Diana's open window where he rubbed against the screen, peered into the dim chaos of her room, and meowed urgently. His mistresses were away.

The animals were hungry and, as creatures will do, took matters into their own hands. They forgot about commitments and promises. They forgot about the source of their well-being. As Toad would tell it, a spirit of harlotry overtook their hearts.

No one would say where the baby birds came from. We found them lying side by side in a pool of blood before the back door. Their tiny wings were folded over small naked bodies. Isabella Hephzibah, the rabbit, turned her back on the scene in horror. Her companion, Captain Midnight, made himself a small dark ball in the recesses of his hutch. Toad testified that he had seen the two cats bowing before the figures with his own eyes before the dew had dried on the sweet peas. He said he cried out a warning, but that a spirit of harlotry had taken over the cats and closed their minds to the law. Later the cats would blame the dog, who said over and over that he was in his pen the whole time being a good dog, and didn't he deserve a treat for that?

"PEOPLE ARE KISSING COWS!" Can you name the source of this quotation?

(1) The headline in a supermarket tabloid: "Mysterious New Disease Makes People Fall in Love with Cows. Oprah And Jacko May Be Victims!"

(2) Bizarre guests on a daytime talk show: "No one knew about our hidden life in the pasture."

(3) Tonight's featured story on "Sixty Minutes": "Strange Cult Welcomes Second Millennium with Bovine Worship."

The answer is none of the above. You remember. It's from that minor prophet with marital troubles, Hosea. He married a woman who was a prostitute. She left him for a lover, but he brought her back. Hosea's grief and anguish over his wife's betrayal gave him an uncanny insight into God's own heartache over the faithlessness of the people of Israel. Hosea knew what it was like to have a false-hearted lover, and his painful experience fueled his passionate eloquence on behalf of the Lord.

Hosea was the first prophet to attack idolatry in any thoroughgoing way. Elijah and Elisha prophesied against the worship of Baal, but neither of them objected to the use of pagan symbols, rites, and practices in the worship of Yahweh; as long as one worshiped the Lord, the forms mattered little. Hosea saw that the forms in this instance mattered greatly. One may worship the Lord, but if the kind of worship is not in keeping with the nature of that Lord, then one really is not worshiping the Lord at all. For Hosea, as for the more recent prophet, Marshall McLuhan, the medium was the message. Forms, rituals, symbols, all carry implicit theological meanings. Hosea believed something other than novelty, political correctness, and the whims of popular opinion ought to inform worship.

Hosea prophesied in a time that sounds much like our own. The nation was arrogant, shortsighted, and blind to the severity of its situation. The political corruption was matched in severity with the corruption of moral and ethical behavior. Because of this the land mourned. All who lived in the land languished, the wild animals and the birds of the air. Even the fish of the sea were perishing.

Hosea declared that there was no faithfulness or loyalty and no knowledge of God in the land. The expression *knowledge of God* implies an intimate relationship in which an individual has made a serious effort to study God's nature, how God operates in the creation, and what God's requirements of us are. Hosea's prophetic vision cut through the deceit of his time to name precisely the sin of the people:

> My people inquire of a thing of wood, and their staff gives them oracles. For a spirit of harlotry has led them astray, and they have left their God to play the harlot. They sacrifice on the tops of mountains, and make offerings upon the hills, under oak, poplar, and terebinth, because their shade is good (4:11–13b).

While Israel gave lip service to Yahweh, she actually took over the whole pagan Canaanite cult with its immorality and lewdness. The people had lost their trust in the Lord and become yoked to idols. Hosea saw that our real god is not the god we worship but the god we serve. This calf that people were kissing was set up in the reign of Jeroboam for convenience and expediency, two powerful contemporary gods: "Whereupon the king took counsel, and made two calves of gold, and said unto them, 'It is too much for you to go to Jerusalem: Behold thy gods, O Israel'" (1 Kings 12:28).

Idolatry, the worship of gods other than the one living true God, continues to maintain its grip on human hearts. An idol, which may be materialistic, intellectual, or spiritual, is whatever we let run the show in our lives that is not God. An idol is what I have more faith in than God. It may be money, success, or more subtle notions we carry in our heads and before which we bow.

An idol may reveal its presence in the pain I feel when I am suddenly deprived of it, because idolatry is a form of addiction. Its hold on me can be very difficult to break. I look to the idol for something I need to feel whole and good about myself. I organize my life, my efforts, my hopes and dreams, around the idol. I sacrifice for it and serve it with my money and my passion.

Idols, which enslave us and demand obeisance, may make themselves known in our stress and despair. They deceive. At first we may think we are getting exactly what we want. Yet over time they show their true colors. They are merciless and insatiable, always demanding more and more of us. They suck the life out of us and, in the end, they leave us feeling worthless, empty, and without joy or hope.

An idol may also signal its presence in confusion, inner conflict, tension, and doubt. We find ourselves divided, double minded, and pulled this way and that. It may show up in our drivenness and how upset we become when things do not go as we want. We may find it in our anxiety and irritability and need to be in control.

Idols exalt the power of my will and foster self-centeredness. Idolatry represents a retreat from the ambiguity and tension of human freedom and the reality of the limitations of this world. An idol saves me from taking responsibility for my existence in God. It subverts the difficult developmental tasks of adult maturation and insults my intelligence. Idols excuse me from entering the pain and isolation of being a separate being in a world of separate beings and coming to terms with evil, sin, and human limits.

In Jesus Christ, God has shown us the way for becoming fully human, a way that does not circumvent the painful realities of sin and evil but asks us to follow Christ right through the heart of them to new life.

As we grow in love with God and our commitment becomes stronger, the idols we serve become subtler, but just as tenacious. Thomas Green writes that the function of the dark night of the spiritual journey is the purgation of such deeper idolatry:

> But there are deeper attachments, more subtle and harder to
> root out, which we begin to discover only when we are already
> committed to the Lord: the attachment to my own ideas about
> how God should be working in me and through me, the deeper
> vanity disguised as zeal.[45]

Some sins we can remove on our own. Others God must first reveal to us and assist in their removal. Still others are rooted so deeply in our psyches with fragile twisting filaments that major surgery is required. The dark night is a time for such surgery. God sets about to set us free from something we may not even recognize has us in chains. Our reaction may be to cry bloody murder, throw ourselves down on the ground, and kick our legs. Or we may pout and sulk, covet our neighbors, become bitter and resentful. We may mourn and feel the sharp sting of betrayal. All of this is a pretty sure sign that whatever it is we are not getting our way about is an idol we have served in one way or another.

The lure of idolatry lies partly in our inability to wait for the Lord. In a world that prizes instant gratification, idolatry finds many converts. It was while the people were waiting for Moses to come down from Sinai that they got into trouble with another cow. Their anxiety built over forty days and forty nights. "When the people saw that Moses delayed to come down from the mountain, they gathered around Aaron and said to him, 'Come make gods for us, who shall go before us, as for this Moses, the man who brought us up out of the land of Egypt we do not know what has become of him.'" So Aaron took gold from the people and formed it in a mold and cast an image of a calf. Later when the irate Moses confronted him, Aaron feebly explained, "I said who ever has gold, take it off, so they gave it to me, and I threw it into the fire, and out came this calf!" (Exod. 32:1, 23–24). Gosh, Moses, it just appeared!

Idols are like that. They seem to take on a life of their own as we distance ourselves from any responsibility for their existence in our lives.

Much of the spiritual journey is taken up with waiting, where the task is simply to trust and obey. At first we may rebel, go astray, and fall prey to idols, but, oddly, after a time we may discover we prefer the waiting with our wills surrendered, dwelling in mystery, watching our life in God unfold. We begin to become suspicious of too much consolation and the roller coaster ride of experience. We are becoming refined to appreciate the subtle essence of God. We come to prefer God to the consolations of God. We may discover there is more than enough of God in one flower petal to keep us engaged in wonder and gratitude for a lifetime. A world and a religion which grab and seek to possess God, which wallow in sensation, and which lust after feeling will have less and less appeal.

Then we can return to the Lord with Hosea's words of repentance. Take away all our guilt. Foreign alliances and idols will not save us. "We will say no more, 'Our God,' to the work of our hands" (14:3).

"OH TOAD, you pious old stick in the mud," said Seal, batting him with her paw. "This is the latest thing. These birds are presents, tender and young, for our beloved Lady. Two for her! This will bring us many favors. This will prove what wonderful cats we are. We will have breakfast on time and many special treats. Surely our heads will be anointed with many pettings and we will dwell in the house of our mistress all the days of their lives."

Toad puffed himself out and hopped up on the bench. "You idiots with your half-baked notions. Cats, you have deeply corrupted yourselves! The Lady desires steadfast love and not sacrifice."

That evening a full moon rose in the heaven and hung over the pear tree like a silver plate. The deck had been swept, the baby birds buried, the cats scolded. Blue Jay flew down to a branch of the pear tree and screeched, "Bad cats! Bad cats!" Just then the crickets swelled, and Toad hopped out of the sweet pea vines to the sidewalk. Strumming a tiny guitar, in a gravelly voice like Bob Dylan he began to sing:

You may be a tomcat a struttin' in the night,
You may be a tabby with a coat so bright,
You may be a house cat a-sleepin' on a bed,
You may be a pedigreed with ribbons on your head.

But you're gonna have to serve somebody.
Yeah, you're gonna have to serve somebody.

The rabbits thumped the bass on the deck with their hind feet. The mourning doves cooed, "Oowah, oowah." The locusts revved up the treble. Then Blue Jay and the crickets wailed in back up, *Serve somebody!* Toad croaked on with a nasal twang:

Well, it may be the devil, or it may be the Lord,
But you're going to have to serve somebody. Serve somebody!

Blue Jay and the crickets dipped and swayed to the beat.

You might like some caviar or pistachio ice cream.
Or maybe chopped liver on strawberries is your dream.
You might bow before your belly or kiss a demon's ring.
You can make a god to worship out of anything.
But you're gonna have to serve somebody.
Yeah, you're gonna have to serve somebody.
Serve somebody!

Toad was grooving now. A group of nightcrawlers came up out of the ground to boogie. The two cats were wearing new collars, which gleamed in the moonlight. Seal's was bright yellow. Gavin's was blue. The small gold bells on the collars tinkled in time as they swayed with the beat.

Well it may be the devil or it may be the Lord,
But you're going to have to serve somebody.

PART VII

· · ·

We Have Eternity

$\mathcal{A}$s I showed a guest around the hermitage, we spoke of schedules and getting things done. Turning to go I remarked, "Well, we don't have to worry. We have eternity, you know."

Where did that come from? I wondered as I closed the gate at the end of the lane. We have eternity. Really? Urgency undergirds the Gospels and much of the rest of the New Testament. Time is supposed to be running out. Come quickly, Lord Jesus! Mark uses the word *immediately* thirty-five times in his Gospel, appearing seven times in the first chapter alone. "This treatise explains how to reach divine union quickly," promises John of the Cross in the opening words of his *Ascent to Mount Carmel.*[46] And there is Jesus, straining at the gate, "I have a baptism to be baptized by and would that it were accomplished!" (Luke 12:50).

A Lakota Sioux spiritual leader once came to visit the hermitage. We sat in silence on the porch for a long time listening to the breeze shake the willows. Then he stood and said, "I will leave two prayer songs." We walked to the dock and joined hands with his daughters and my friend. We stood in a circle to send the song to the four directions, as he sang the slow haunting melody given to his people by the White Buffalo Calf Woman. Then, turning to the west, he sang a song of vision to the Great Spirit. When the song was over, we listened as the prayers reverberated in concentric circles into the universe on and on, like ripples moving out from a stone tossed in the pond. "This is the center of the world," he said. "Wherever you pray is the center of the world. There all things begin."

Prayer places us in the center of the world, anchoring us simultaneously in God and in the heart of all that God has made. No matter how remote we are located, prayer puts us in the center of all places. Prayer also centers us outside of time, in eternity.

I STOOD ON A MESA across from the Cerro Pedernal near Abiquiu, New Mexico. To my right tucked in the rugged hills eighteen winding miles up a wilderness canyon was the Monastery of Christ in the Desert. There thirty monks were helping to hold the world together by their simple rhythm of prayer and work. I belonged to that silent world of solitaries. I wanted to be swaddled in the cloth of prayer and praise woven daily by a community of faith or to be attached like an anchorite to a church that understood the ministry of solitude. Below me and to the left stretched the 21,000 acres of Ghost Ranch, a conference center of my denomination. When I knelt for my ordination vows eighteen years ago, I promised to serve this Church with imagination, intelligence, energy, and love. My loved ones were back at the ranch, and the conference center teemed with creative activity, learning, laughter, and hunger for God. Standing on the mesa between those two worlds, I recalled a dream of years ago in which I was giving guided tours of a monastery, interpreting the contemplative life to people looking for God.

"There is a pervasive form of contemporary violence to which . . . we easily succumb: activism and overwork," said Merton. He saw the rush and pressure of modern life as perhaps the most common form of its innate violence. "To allow oneself to be carried away by a multitude of conflicting concerns, to surrender to too many demands, to commit oneself to too many projects, to want to help everyone in everything is to succumb to violence."[47] I have seen the violence that a culture, finding its worth in doing and possessing, does to its own soul. This is the violence that numbs, dulls, and blinds our awareness of the holiness of all that is. This is the violence that spawns violence's children: racism, poverty, injustice, and oppression.

Perhaps the urgency of Mark, St. John of the Cross, Jesus, and others is the hurry to discover that we don't have to hurry. The sooner we see that in Christ we possess eternity, the better. Wherever it was I thought I was going on this slow journey, over and over I discovered I had already arrived. "I am the Alpha and the Omega, the first and the last, the Beginning and the End," says Jesus from the throne.

We are home before we ever leave.

LET'S GO BACK to the beginning of this book. Remember how I was lying on a cot at the hermitage, weak and sick. I lay. I watched the hummingbird. I watched the enthroned Christ. I held the suffering Savior. He slept.

I rose and walked to the dock. Turtles sunned on the rock. Dragon flies and blue damsels danced. Two ducks floated on the east shore. A rabbit sat still in the grass. I walked barefoot in the sand, picking up sticks and twenty-year-old debris left on the shore by drought. I squished my toes in the mud.

I sat on the dock and stretched my neck to the sun with the turtles. The air pulsed with the hum of insects. A breeze blew gently through the willows. Grace was in me and without, and grace was everywhere, and everywhere was grace, and I was grace. And I was home by way of Turtle Street.

1998–1999

CHAPTER 33

The Real World
Futility Rules the Roost

I pull open the gate and walk across the wooden bridge and up the hill to the hermitage. Bluebirds flit through the trees in bright splashes of color. An intricate sticky network of webs festoons my path. Meadowlarks warble from the power line. As I round the corner and start down the slope to the back door, a dozen turtles that had climbed up the sides of a half-submerged boat to sun now splash into the water. With a raspy grawk, a startled heron spreads its huge wings and sweeps across the lake like a gangly primeval gargoyle.

Unlocking the door I pause and sigh on the threshold, "Ah this is the *real* world!" Like those turtles that had plopped into the water, worry and stress drop off me and disappear into the green dark of the lake.

I love the way Eugene Peterson puts it:

> Here is what I want you to do: find a quiet secluded place so that you won't be tempted to role-play before God. Just be there as simply and honestly as you can manage. The focus will shift from you to God, and you will begin to sense his grace.[48]

Holy ground, wherever it is found, is the real world because here is where we can be real. Here is where it is safe and free enough for us to discover and name our reality. And wherever truth is, there is God. "When I shall cleave to Thee with all my being, then shall I in nothing have pain and labor; and my life shall be a real life, being wholly full of Thee," wrote St. Augustine.[49] My life becomes a real life as it fills with God. The Holy One who is Ultimate Reality is known in the holy ground of our own reality.

The journey of faith may be understood as a journey toward greater personal authenticity. Like the Velveteen Rabbit, we become real through a series of losses and reversals. What is artificial and phony in us is gradually revealed and discarded and our lives become real lives full of God rather than our self-conceit and pride.

> One thing, one thing I asked of you that will I seek after. Here is my heart's desire, my deepest longing, and my greatest need: to come where you are staying, to live where you live, to be at home with you day after day. I want to behold your beauty, and to see your face with my own eyes. I want to inquire in your holy place. I want to love you and consider you and your wisdom. (Psalm 27:4, author's paraphrase)

Dwelling in God's house requires us to be ourselves and to resist the temptation to be or to do anything other than that which is authentically us. Here is our high calling as creatures created by God: to discover and set free our own particular version of the image of God. The rabbi tells the student, "When you die and go to heaven, God will not ask, 'Were you Abraham? Were you Moses? Were you Elijah?' God will ask, 'Were you *you*?'"

EARLY IN MY MINISTRY I joined a pastors' study group, a congenial and supportive group of colleagues engaged in parish ministry. One week we read Psalm 27, and it spoke so powerfully of my own longing that tears came to my eyes. I did not know at the time that this verse is sometimes referred to as the contemplative vocation. I soon decided to leave the study group and spend a day each week in prayer and solitude rather than with my colleagues and friends. As much as I enjoyed the study and fellowship, the real me didn't belong in the group. I was amused to discover that what was hardest for me to give up was the gossip and being included in denominational politics and scuttlebutt.

When my daughters were younger, we used to giggle over a book of *Improbable Records*, compiled by Quentin Blake and John Yoeman. One of our favorites was the first inflatable swimming aid, the Bickerstaff Brothers' Buoyancy Bathing Suit for Beginners (1865). Quentin Blake's hilarious illustration showed an alarmed, bearded gentlemen in an inflated striped bathing suit. His arms and legs flailed in the air, while he bounced on top of the waves. The picture reminded me of St. Paul and his description of knowledge, which puffs up, as opposed to love, which builds up.

Many other things can puff us up and leave us bobbing ridiculously in the air like blimps. Pride, for example, inflates us, lifts us high off the ground, and prevents our keeping in touch with what is real and true in our lives. We bounce pompously along on the surface of life, never really swimming in reality. Reality connects us with the earth.

When I was teaching speech at a university, I received an end-of-course evaluation that stunned me. The anonymous student quoted a few sentences from my opening lecture, in which I encouraged students to be themselves, open and honest and real. "'Be real,' she said in her phony voice with her phony advice and studied mannerisms." The student's cynical criticism cut me to the quick. It would be many years before I could see how accurate it was.

Artifice and phoniness that is conscious and contrived are the sort of things that spin doctors coach political leaders in. There is also the less conscious fakery of the false self—a self put on in the aftermath of loss or trauma to hide a truth that seems unacceptable.

One of the barriers to personal authenticity is the pride born of encounter with the inevitable futility of the world. Paul told the Romans that creation was made subject to futility and that it was in bondage to decay by God's own choosing. Isn't that the truth? I bought some auburn hair color the other day to try to disguise some of the signs of my own inexorable slide toward decay. The Greek word translated as "futility," *mataios*, denotes the world of appearance as distinct from that of being. *Mataios* means the absence of effect; it describes what is vain, pointless, foolish. It includes notions of nothingness, running down, disorder, and chaos. Paul is describing something similar to what modern scientists call entropy, the degradation of matter and energy in the universe to an ultimate state of inert uniformity.

The Hebrew correlate of *mataios* used in the Old Testament derives from a word that means "vapor" or "breath" and often connotes idolatry or idols; the word means "that which is not real." Paul tells us the creation is held enslaved to unreality. Our sin may be seen as our desire for nothingness, for that which is ultimately illusory, as insubstantial as the grass that flourishes in the morning and fades and withers at evening.

I have had exasperating days when wherever my eye fell I saw evidence of futility. This is usually on cleaning days—the peeling paint on the woodwork, the worn linoleum, the screen door with the holes that let in flies, the weeds in the flower garden and overgrown shrubs, the unanswered correspondence, the trash on the porch, the stained wallpaper where the roof leaked . . . Far from dwelling in the house of the Lord and beholding God's beauty, I find myself helplessly trapped in a world that is falling apart. Paul reminds me that I and all that is in creation are subject to frustration, breakdowns, breakups, erosions, defeats, and setbacks by—*get this*—God's own will. This is the way God wants it.

Paul explains it like this: "For while we live, we are always being given up to death for Jesus' sake, so that the life of Jesus may be made visible in our mortal flesh. So death is at work in us, but life in you" (2 Cor. 4:11-12). Humankind and the rest of creation are engaged in a perpetual remodeling and maintenance project, a real estate permanent "fixer-upper." We are like the laundry in our household, never done. Futility rules the roost, as any homemaker knows who has run the sweeper and dusted the same table over and over. As Edna St. Vincent Millay observed: "It is not true that life is one damn thing after another—it's one damn thing over and over."[50]

This is the world we live in, the world God made, where evil prowls at the door waiting for a chance to pounce, where corruption is established in high and low places; and where we expend huge amounts of energy trying to halt our predestined skid toward disintegration.

Yet, bad as things appear to be, awareness of the futility and unreality of creation holds the possibility of *real* life. Initially our encounters with the futility of creation may increase our self-deception and pride and create barriers to personal authenticity. Sin, our desire for the unreal and our idolatrous seeking after the ephemeral, leads to the injury and the pride that alienate us from our true selves and from God.

The false self is created out of the lies we tell ourselves and others when we come up against ridicule, neglect, abuse, and the death that is at work in us. We feel great pain, sadness, anger, but we pretend we are all right. We begin to act a role. We hide and deny our truth for a dozen different reasons. Maybe we are ashamed and feel our pain is our fault. Maybe we have no one trustworthy to whom we can tell our truth. Maybe we have been frightened into silence. Whatever the reason, we begin to present a false face to the world about something of great significance to us.

To doubt the truth of our own experience is a profound betrayal, an act of self-alienation. So we struggle not only with creation's bondage to decay but also with our betrayal of the truth of our experience with that decay and futility.

The psalmist asks one thing of the Lord. If you were to ask one thing of God, what would it be? This fellow goes for the gold. Following the poetic form of repetition, he actually asks for three things, variants of the one thing: to dwell in the house of God forever, to behold the beauty of God, to inquire in God's temple. These three comprise the one thing: an intimate abiding with God which involves seeing God's beauty and engaging in conversation and inquiry with God. That is what I want, says the psalmist. And that is only what I want.

In contrast, Martha tells Jesus that she wants him to make Mary help her with the meal preparation. I can identify with Martha. I am often distracted with much serving, and I come to Jesus like a whining sibling tattletale. "Make these people help me. See all I am trying to do. There is so much to do. It's not fair. Do something Lord." I want God to help me accomplish my agenda.

Jesus looks at this worn-out woman and says, "Martha, Martha, your service has distracted you from what is really important. There is one thing necessary. Mary has chosen the better part. She has set aside her own agenda for intimate communion with me."

Martha, get real. You are engaged in a vain struggle with a futile creation.

What a shock it must have been for Martha to hear this. I bet she was madder than a wet hen. I sure would be. Isn't that just like a man who has no idea what goes into keeping a house, preparing a meal, or caring for children?

I have a Martha in me, dishrag in hand, sleeves rolled up to conquer the futility of creation, who looks with suspicion and disapproval upon my inner Mary. And my Mary finds Martha overbearing and scary in her never-ending bustling and fixing and overfunctioning. On the surface of things, Mary has little to show for her efforts. There are no rows of canned tomatoes in the cellar or piles of neatly folded laundry. Yet over and over she is drawn to stop and seat herself before wonder, something larger and wiser and more beautiful than she. She turns aside from the vain world's distractions for what? Just what is the necessary thing?

Saint John of the Cross and others call it holy idleness or contemplation. Brenda Ueland, in her wonderful book *If You Want to Write*, calls it "moodling":

> So you see imagination needs moodling—long, inefficient, happy idling, dawdling and puttering. These people who are always briskly doing something and are as busy as waltzing mice, they have little, sharp, staccato ideas, such as: "I see where I can make an annual cut of $3.47 in my meat budget." But they have no slow, big ideas. And the fewer consoling, noble, shining, free, jovial, magnanimous ideas that come, the more nervously and desperately they rush and run from office to office and up and down stairs, thinking by action at last to make life have some warmth and meaning.[51]

177

The story of Mary and Martha, which occurs only in Luke, follows the parable of the Good Samaritan. Luke's point may be that love and service to neighbor is not enough, indeed that it is possible to be distracted with much serving. When we are anxious and troubled with many things, we do not give effective service. We waste our efforts and time doing things that are not necessary. We lose the perspective and vision of Christ. Service is valuable only as it flows from our communion with the living word.

A sure sign of God's care and love is that futility, the very godlessness of creation, and being a finite being cast into a world on the road to ruin drive us to contemplation—to the real world where Christ awaits us. When we come to an impasse where we see the futility of our lives, linear analytic thinking comes to a halt. We stop exhausted, unable to come up with solutions or answers. This leads us into contemplation and activates the right side of the brain. Our imagination is forced to move more deeply into our experience in the search for meaning and truth.

And truth, whether we recognize it as such or not, always brings us to the feet of Christ.

CHAPTER 34

Waiting
Broccoli and Perseverance

Gold coins scattered across blue sky
Wind shaking the pear tree
Limbs twisting, bending
Coins shuddering down in spatters of light.
By day's end not one leaf remains upon a branch.
At dusk dark scribbles on heaven's vault
Spell in grotesque script,
"Let go. Let go."

Isabella Hephzibah, a rabbit with an eye on eternity, sits in her cage stretched out in the December sun. She lost the vision in her left eye after an injury. Now one eye looks out on the world while the other is turned to an inscrutable realm we cannot enter. The cats snooze nearby in their basket. Isabella's dark brother, Captain Midnight, presses his nose against her cage. They have been nibbling pear leaves and twigs. Isabella Hephzibah, whose name means "beautiful one, my delight is in her," is doing what she does best, waiting. She is still and quiet as she watches at the door.

A friend of mine is also waiting. Recently she asked me for the key to success in surviving a child's thirteenth year. She told me she ate some truly nasty broccoli at dinner one night in a desperate attempt to do something good for herself. She swallowed the stuff in the hope that it would help her live long enough to see her son become the parent of a thirteen-year-old.

Longevity and sheer perseverance have a lot to do with justice and salvation. If you can live long enough, you just may see the triumph of good.

Being able to hang on, to wait through periods when all seems turned against you, to survive and prevail is a central activity of a Christian.

Some pastors struggle to get congregations to sing the more somber and penitential Advent hymns before the favorite Christmas carols. I am not surprised. Our culture's mindless celebration of Christmas distorts the basic truth of the season, namely, our need for redemption and what might be required of us to receive it. We gloss over our appalling sin and ruin, skip past the eager groan of creation's need for healing. We drug ourselves against the suffering of dark nights. We grow numb and fall asleep before the TV instead of keeping alert and obedient watch for God's saving action in our lives. We succumb to the temptation to consume more and more as we race to gratify desires.

In contrast, Christ tells us that here is where we are to linger, to stay awake, to wait and be ready, here in the bleak and barren heart of our need.

Timing is everything. Should one push, move ahead and make something happen, or lay low, wait, and watch for the hand of the Lord to act? Tolerating ambiguity, not knowing and uncertainty, can be excruciating. In our anxiety and fear we may take things into our own hands. As a general rule of discernment, when in doubt, wait. The stance of faith waits, trusts, praises, and gives thanks. Faith joined with love bears all things, believes all things, hopes all things, and endures all things. Why is that hard for us? Perhaps we fear that we won't be vindicated, that our longing will not be fulfilled, that our cause will not be redeemed, that things will not be made right and goodness will not prevail.

My friend with the thirteen-year-old told me her family motto: "Learn to bear what must be borne." This stern admonition carried for me a puritanical severity—a life of gritted teeth, pursed lips, and making the best of one trial after another. But when I shared the proverb with another friend, "What a great theme for Advent," she exclaimed, seeing a possibility I had missed. My understanding shifted from regarding what must be borne as some heavy load and having to slog along through life like a drudge to the exhilarating task of the labor and delivery of a baby.

Like the Butterfly McQueen character in the film *Gone with the Wind*, when it comes to difficult tasks, I have tended to overestimate my strength and courage. When faced with reality, I cower and snivel, "But Miss Scarlet, I don't know nothin' 'bout birthin' no babies!"

"Love in action is a harsh and dreadful thing compared to love in dreams,"[52] observed Dostoevsky. The Advent season invites us into the harsh and dreadful task of giving birth to a love that will ask more of us than we thought we could bear. Learning to bear the one who must be born, the Christ, into our lives, families, communities, and world requires us to wait, persevere, and overcome fear with faith.

The Promise

> How long can you carry a secret, a gift of saving love before giving birth to it? How long can you ponder things in your heart and sit on the stone path in the sun? After a while it becomes obvious that there is something up your sleeve, or under your tunic. Someone's delight is in you and is growing bigger every day.

Some us are called to bear children. All of us, male and female, are called to give birth to Christ. We each carry God's seed, a divine promise in us and for us. Each is called to conceive some aspect of the great promise of salvation, to surrender to it, to carry and nourish it and give it birth on its terms in its time. Here we are at the service of powers greater than we are. We find ourselves as servants and handmaids, those who stand alert and ready at the door for the one they serve, who may come at any time. We belong to the promise and are given over to the promise. The child of the promise is the unique offering you and only you can give out of your love in the Bethlehem of your life.

What is it? Who is it? How is this done? We are each alone here. There were no witnesses when Gabriel came. One or two may understand, who are strong when we are weak, who have hope when we have despair, who have faith when we have none. For the most part we must face the rejection, fears, doubts, and devils alone. And then, suddenly in the dark, comes the sharp all-encompassing pain of labor—so much more painful than we had ever imagined it could be.

It may not look like all that much, your child and your offering of yourself as the mother of redemption. It may seem a small thing compared to Mary's child. The child you bear may be nothing more (or less) than the courage to get through a bad day, or a shred of hope you cling to like a broken raft in the midst of a churning sea.

Two signs may help you tell if this is your Christ child: your vision of the joy or beauty or love set free in the gift you offer; and your sacrificial suffering in the labor and delivery of that gift. Such suffering is not a consequence of abuse or injustice. This is the suffering of love firmly grounded in Christ which is assailed by evil as it seeks to remain firm in its faith in the efficacy and power of God's suffering love on the cross.

> *Waiting, waiting—how did she keep the promise alive, the hope, the word which was spoken to her, through all the days and nights while she walked the rocky paths? What good could come out of Nazareth? How can this be? I have no husband. I have no money. I have no strength. I have no hope. I have no skill . . . But he said, Nothing is impossible with God . . . A secret between her and the angel, a child growing in a hostile environment and stillness at dusk when the light slides under the horizon leaving a golden smear of hushed anticipation. She was like a tiny flame in a sea of darkness.*

The Threats

Maybe there will be a miscarriage. Maybe the child will be ill or damaged. Maybe nothing will happen, and I have made this all up. The demons slink in through our wounds, our past hurts and losses, and taunt, harass, confuse, lie, and distort. Feeding on our fear, they float in our minds like bloated carcasses.

Impatience fueled by fear and lack of faith has caused many an aborted Christ child. Some dreams are wrenched too soon from the womb of God's providence to die torn and bleeding in the back rooms of our souls. Fearing that the Promised One cannot be trusted to save us from ourselves, we join the tribe of those who attempt to seize the kingdom by violence.

The promise always comes in the context of threats, writes biblical scholar Walter Brueggemann.

> The land of promise is never an eagerly waiting vacuum antici-pating Israel. Nor is it an unambiguous arena for faith. It is always filled with Canaanites. That is how the promise comes . . . It is the very land of promise, the purpose of the whole journey of faith, which causes the failure of nerve. . . .
>
> God's people always want to settle for something short of promises, because promises fulfilled remind Israel how vulner-able it is, how exposed it is, and how precarious it all is. Promiseless existence is safer. The Bible knows from the begin-ning that promises are always kept in the midst of threats. Tables are always prepared "in the presence of my enemies" and

if one would eat at the table, one must eat in the presence of enemies. The land is precisely for those and only for those who sense their precariousness and act in their vulnerability.[53]

Threats in whatever form they come tend to scare the wits out of us. We feel like puny grasshoppers compared to these giants. Possibly the greatest threat, according to Jesus, is the failure to believe, the lack of faith. There is that time before the pregnancy shows and no one can tell what is inside, and even after one has something visible to point to, like a vision, a possibility, the first faint glimmerings of a new idea, when the actual outcome is shrouded in mystery and the course of the life of the new one to be born is unknown to us. So there is a lot of holding-onto, of nourishing the invisible, the inklings, and the suggestions—the voice of some ethereal visitor who spoke of something wondrous and unbelievable.

Who could you tell? What would they think? Maybe your lover will understand and give his support. Maybe God will intervene in a dream. Maybe a wise old friend whose own promise leaps in recognition of your promise, maybe the old cousin will understand.

But there is a long time of hours, days, months, and even years—year upon year—when much is hidden and only you sing in your heart of what is to come, the gift you will offer. And what to do until then? Fall back on praise and being. Notice the leaf in the redbud tree outside your window, curled and brown, crisp in the sun. Stand at sundown as the earth grows still and silence creeps into the hermitage like a cat and curls at your feet and purrs.

"Blessed is she who believed that the word of the Lord would be fulfilled," says the cousin. Blessed are those who believe in the glad and amazing truth that sings in their hearts, trusting with Mary and her Son that all will be well and that they are highly favored.

The Surrender

The earth, muffled with snow, goes about its hidden preparation for spring. Silence spreads over the land. Our pace slows with the burden we are blest to bear. The angel with his face of fire and his wings is now a dim memory. God has become a long, low hum, a slow pulsing throb. We are like the inside of a struck gong vibrating peace. The fox in the woods stops in its tracks and sits up listening—still. The hawk on the wing wheels in a broad circle, glides down a current, and settles on the post—still. The chickadee at the feeder stops, tilts its head listening—still. Isabella, opens her eyes and lifts her ears—still.

Then with no warning it comes. Wrenching pain seizes us like a sword in the belly. We collapse to our knees and crouch in the darkness in terror. Impaled by the circumstances of our lives and God's call to us, we writhe on the cross with Jesus. Extended far beyond our feeble powers, such bearing is more than we can do. With each new contraction we lose our nerve and cower like Peter saying, "We don't know nothin' 'bout no man named Savior."

Now we may recall Jesus' question, "Are you able to drink the cup that I drink, or be baptized with the baptism that I am baptized with?" And we had boasted like idiots, "We are able!" We had no idea what would be asked. Now between contractions we pray, "If it be your will, remove this cup from me. But not my will, but yours."

To entrust ourselves to the will of God at the very moment when we feel most alone, most rejected, and in the most pain requires us to have come to the absolute end of our own will and resources. What makes such a thing possible? How could Mary persevere? How did Paul in prison and facing death continue to preach the gospel? Perhaps it was their surrender, their sense that something larger than themselves had taken hold of them. An ax had been laid at their roots. A furious whirlwind had shaken and blasted them. Now all in them that was chaff was burning in an unquenchable fire. Finally exhausted from resisting they say, "Yes, yes. You are in charge. You are God. I love you. I trust you. I don't like or even understand this, but I give myself to you however you want me. My will and desires die to yours."

A birth is not something one does as much as submits to. Processes set in motion long ago now come to fuller expression. One's being is given over to a life and purpose beyond itself. The best thing to do is simply to hold still, breathe with the pain, and wait between contractions.

The Greek word used in the Bible for wait is *hypomenein*. It means "to stay behind, to stand still, to hold out." *Hypomenein* includes in its nuances to cleave to God in simple, quiet confident waiting as well as to endure, stand fast, persevere; and it includes courageous active resistance to hostile attack.

Wait in the New Testament refers to the endurance that is given for the realization of the kingdom. It is the basic attitude of the Christian as we face the attacks of a hostile and unbelieving world and as we find ourselves in the midst of temptations. The power to persevere is drawn from faith and hope.

Will, knowledge, technology have no power to bring about salvation, wrote Simone Weil.

The role of humanity is to wait . . . The attitude that brings about salvation is not like any form of activity. . . . It is the waiting or attentive and faithful immobility that lasts indefinitely and cannot be shaken. The slave, who waits near the door so as to open immediately when the master knocks, is the best image of it. He must be ready to die of hunger and exhaustion rather than change his attitude . . .We just have to wait for the solution. . . . Seeking leads us astray. This is the case with every form of what is truly good. [We] should do nothing but wait for the good and keep evil away.[54]

Might you be entrusted with a task to match the largeness of your soul? Could you, like Mary, tell your cousin, "My soul magnifies the Lord, and my spirit rejoices in God my savior, for he has looked with favor on the lowliness of his servant"? Is such heroism only for martyrs in foreign lands, prophets defying oppressive governments, and saints whose lives trace truth in their own blood?

THE DOOR OPENED at last. Footsteps moved toward her. Isabella turned her head and sat up. She heard the familiar greeting, "Oh you beautiful one, my delight is in you!" She stretched her neck as fingers rubbed under her chin ruff. Soon a large red apple appeared before her. She bit off a big chunk and chewed. The sweet juice filled her throat. The sun warmed her back and her heart swelled with joy.

If you are summoned by an angel, if you find your heart stretched big with some unnameable love with a mind of its own, eat your broccoli. Exercise. Take your vitamins. Floss and wait. Ask Isabella. It will be worth it just to be around on the day of the Lord, however long it takes.

CHAPTER 35

Time Tripping
Dancing with the Risen Lord

O Risen One, O Death Defied!
You are the immaculate apprehension of the place beyond tension
known in the unknowing, beheld in the letting go,
met on the nuptial bed of ultimate repose and ultimate fecundity
in the union of the still pond and the day star
where the million dancing diamonds
and the thousand and one things are conceived.

Come Brilliance, come Pulse, come Fire
into quiet depth, cool darkness.
There at the point of entry, where the heart is held open with a feather,
where the foot is placed upon the surface of the sea,
there—before sun swallowed becomes green dark,
before water drawn rises to heat, dissolving into light—
there now on the trembling membrane of Love
place your foot, your palm, your mind
and you will walk on water,
the sea will part, dead rise,
and the wounded made whole.

*M*ight I remain poised there long enough to speak your name one day, gaze upon your face, and touch your palm with perfect love? Could I impose my being upon another's being with the sublime grace of this meeting place?

I have eons to work on it.

Meanwhile, I hear the sound of Love crashing over me like waves, like wind on wheat. I, bowing, kneeling over and over, fold into the earth. And the former foundations crumble. And not one stone upon a stone remains of the limits that hold me holding you. And your seed sings in me. And over and over we tumble, a golden hoop without beginning, without end, arousing joy, pouring ourselves out for the joy, filling ourselves up for the joy, rolling like a wedding band over the land catching freedom.

There are not enough days of raindrops splashing opalescent on the pond, or days of thunder splitting silence into charred strips, or days of snow driven across the field in ghostly sheets, or days of sun and water-blue-sky brilliance, or days of grasshoppers erupting like green geysers before our step, or days of simple tasks, or days of labor, or days of woe, or days and days to sing your praise. So I leave days behind and flesh and time to meet you, smiling on the threshold of each new moment, where you beckon me to follow you from death to life. And we trip time and send it sprawling, spreading in tiny grains, disappearing down the porous floor of heaven, and watering earth with the rhythmic comfort of sequence.

The Ancient of Days

Once upon a time, or under it, in a place beneath the linear reach of mind, in the tiny cupboards in the pantry of experience (first this then this then this then this), we wanted time to tell, to justify the wait, to repair the shredded hope we watered, to redeem the passings past, and to fashion futures dreamed. And we, crouched in our sorrow, cried: *I know my redeemer lives and I shall see his face in the land of the living!* (Job 19:25).

Buy some time or, better, take time. Either we take or are taken—hauled off frayed and bloody in its jaws where it will gnaw us senseless. The preacher says we have eternity in our minds, stuck there like a shard of crystal next to the pineal gland, a transmitter sending and receiving intimations of immortality.

> I have seen the business that God has given to everyone to be
> busy with. God has made everything beautiful in its time; God
> also has put eternity into their minds. (Ecclesiastes 2:10-11)

Sooner or later time runs out and settles like dust over our inarticulate bones. And the only one who can do the talking then shouts, "You hypocrites! You know how to read the signs with your chronometers, barometers, and monitors, but you do not know what time it is! I say to you, before Abraham was I am!" It is a real dilemma. We've got time on our hands and eternity on the brain.

"It's about time," the preacher says, cynical from having seen too much time and spent too much time at committee meetings, potluck suppers, funerals, hospital beds, having strode resolutely down too many passages where trite words were tromped out to fill time.

You've got to learn to tell time where to get off; get over trying to stop it. There is nothing new under the sun. It's all been done before. So grow old, get wrinkled, gray, and stooped.

A VERY OLD WOMAN moved in next door, and almost all she ever said was, "Wee. Wee. Wee." It sounded like a cross between a sneeze and a squeal. She was always about to breathe her last and die, and then she would think better of it and get the giggles. I suppose she'll live forever. She made good oatmeal cookies and fed them to the squirrels. She never brought in her mail, and she let the newspapers pile up in her yard. When we took them to her door, she reached out her arms and held the papers like babies and rocked them saying, "Oh, yes, yes, the world, the world."

At night you could see her heart. It burned like a flame in the dark.

Once some Jehovah's Witnesses went to her door. "We've seen! We've seen!" they said.

"What?" she hollered. "I don't hear well."

And she muttered, "I am the Ancient of Days."

You Can't Have a Good Time

Fly time. Tie it to a string and run over the prairie with it in tow, until it catches the current and glides with the hawks. Make it dip. Feel it tug and lift you from the earth. Reel it in when the wind dies, and carry it in your pocket.

This was why we were so anxious and in such a hurry. We thought that there wouldn't be enough time, that next time wouldn't come, that time would never hold all the adoration in our hearts, that this time would be the last, that time was running out, that we, dodging the clouds, darting like dragonflies over the still pond, would miss the time of our lives.

We thought that joy had to do with time, could be held in time, could be had in time. So we reached for it. But joy has nothing to do with time; and you cannot *have* a good time, you can only *be* it.

The sin was trying to stop time, instead of letting it flow like sand, letting it sift through us—our bodies, clear glass bottles, so that anyone could tell by looking at us what time it was and whose time it was. Time running through us smooth and quick like silent flocks of birds rising, rippling, turning in the soul's serene boundaries.

From the tree the serpent said, "Eat and you will know. Then you will have it all in mind and be able to stand the time it takes to hold your place in line." So we did. We grabbed some time, gobbled it. We made lists, prioritized. We got journals, logs, appointment books, and calendars. We knew and knew. We grew fat on knowing. We ate books swollen with knowledge, and waddled next to each other nosing at the trough.

Yet you stood beyond knowing, eternally opening your arms to us. You, who fractured time, who held it open with your body in the rupture, a marker in the book of ages, spoke to us just in time: "I am the way and the truth and the life. Lo, I will be with you always, even to the end of time."

Our task is to follow the lead of One who dances with us in eternity to music unheard, in a dimension unknown, while we simultaneously waltz here, separating just so we can meet again. Saying, hello, I love you, and good-bye. Touching, releasing. Playing the friction of our distinction. Teasing anticipation. Awakening gladness. Knowing all along we are everlastingly joyfully joined.

To Praise or Perish

"Ask and you shall receive," you promised. You were in our hands like a salve, a balm for all wounds. Healing in our palms, abundance on our lips, "We are not worthy," we said.

Matter resists its spiritualization, rebels, sulks, and protests. The flesh sags under the gravity of its own extremity. Here at the limits of the known world, mortality balks, whinnies, and will go no further.

"Is this what remains after our offering?" we asked. One mute blood-stained altar bridging the gash that wedges torment in the heart of things? We lifted our little hands to heaven. "Here, use me, use me," we prayed.

When we see how truly useless we are, how totally unable to lift a finger to turn the tide, when we crawl on our knees to you and ask for mercy, then you do it. You do it all. And we are dead. All that protests and whines and has to know and to prevail meets its last enemy, not death, but you who conquered death and whose power is made perfect in our weakness.

The choice is adoration or annihilation, to praise or perish. The way is narrow and the margin slim.

It's Time

It's time—time to get up, time to go, time for resurrection. A snail, the color of stones, makes its way across the sidewalk, taking its time reaching into space with dewy tendrils of anticipation. I let it taste my thumb. Sour. Its moist finger recedes.

I suppose we die and are reborn when we can finally stand it, when we can tolerate the heart of variety without falling into fear and having to ask questions about it, having to form opinions, to shroud ourselves with judgments, having to think and feel and test the odors of reality, and ask, What next? What next? What next?

Then we know what our bones know, what the still pond and the pear tree know. Then we know that we will never have to stop loving. That nothing in heaven or on earth can defeat this love and that time is on our side, death is our servant, and annihilation is the mother of adoration.

Released from the bondage of diminishment, we become plenitude, and magnify that which enlarges us. Creation ceases her groaning and, wearing us like a crown of jewels, joins in the happy chorus, rejoicing that neither death nor life nor things present nor things to come will be able to separate us from this love. And the cruel tyranny of days is vanquished. And we, who have been made for this devotion and for this alone, exalt and fall down in wonder, singing liberty:

> When we have come ten thousand years,
> bright shining as the sun,
> we've no less days to sing your praise
> than when we first begun.[55]

It is surrender and surrender and surrender once again. Fling yourself into the moment. Free-fall into the arms of the Risen One. It is playing chicken roaring down Main Street in a '55 Chevy, throttle wide open, hurtling into one's own likeness.

Lose everything but your nerve. "Who do you think you are?" they will ask. "She sure has a lot of nerve," they will say. "What makes him think he has the right?"

Here, I give myself to you. The dowry is meager. My fathers and mothers have always been poor, scraping together a living, never able to get much ahead before a tumult, disaster, or war. I have only this empty chest of hope. I bring you my nothingness, my need, my common lower-class manners, my poor-side-of-town customs, my violence and sin.

There is no way I can be worthy, that I can enter you without defiling you, can touch you without abusing you, or offer shelter wholly pure and chaste and beautiful. So have mercy. Christ, have mercy.

Step Easy

We ordered some nets that were for freeing, not catching. They were made of big, round hoops, the color of gold, and came with magic words: *You are freed of your affliction. You are forgiven. Walk in the name of Jesus. Go and sin no more.* The way they worked was you took something that was caught or imprisoned, and swooped over it with this hoop. Then it was freed.

If you had something stuck somewhere, a piece of bread caught in your throat or a thorn in your heart, you passed this hoop over and rabbits sprang out of cages, rivers gushed over falls, and the dead rose.

How many ways can you say it? *Repent for the kingdom is at hand.*

You can give people a hoop but you can't make them use it.

When the Beloved dies for the Creator, when Love gives itself to the sinner, when Life, diving into the dark, opens its throat and gulps and its sweet cavities suck in the waters of death, there at the meeting place of what is with what will be, we awaken. And the beginning and the end are one.

Perhaps one day in an instant of grace I will love you perfectly. For the time being, I practice, washing my cup, brushing my daughter's golden hair. I step easy over the earth. I redeem with my breath.

I am yours in the Easter of each new moment.

CHAPTER 36

Beauty
Christ Winking at Us through Creation

On the afternoon of the day my friend died in a hospital bed in Iowa City, Diana and I made cookies. In the Kansas kitchen overlooking the finch feeder, while seventeen finch gobbled two pounds of thistle seed (95¢ a pound at Allen Farm and Feed), we measured flour and brown sugar, butter and ginger, and mixed them in the yellow bowl. Patting out the dough on the cookie sheet, we stopped to taste. "Umm, very good!" Diana said.

There, while she stood on the orange chair with a brown apron hanging to her ankles, I saw for the first time how the smooth curve of her cheek presses against space with such exquisite beauty.

DIANA, NOW SEVENTEEN, stands tall and slender in her prom dress before the mirror, fussing with her hair. Rock music blasts from the radio. Cicelia squints as she carefully applies eye shadow; she has been getting ready all day: trial applications of various shades of nail polish, a trip to our neighbor's to borrow long white gloves, phone calls to friends for earnest consultations about the nuances of hairstyle, and considerable angst over how the cream-colored shoes do not quite match the white-silver dress. When appointed hairdressers failed to create the expected effect, both daughters narrowly avert disaster with impromptu stylists.

My husband and I—we watch them coming down the stairs to greet their shy dates, who hold plastic cartons of wrist corsages. Wasn't it just yesterday when they were rummaging in the attic, going through my jewelry box, and hobbling around the house in my old high heels, trailing scarves pretending to do what now they are doing in earnest?

They have been practicing the art of beauty for years, playing Barbies, dressing up, and pouring over piles of *Seventeen* magazines and—from an under-the-bed-stash of contraband—well-read copies of *Cosmo*. How many diary entries of tortured love and longing, how many studied applications of lipstick, have preceded this night? How many poses before the mirror—trying on various attitudes: hair-in-the-eyes adolescent sullen, tanning-bed cheerleader prep, totally valley girl, like for sure, lugubrious Goth, or pink-haired you-can't-make-me punk.

Now the beauties come down the stairs, gowns gracefully trailing behind, looking like strange cousins from abroad, familiar yet wonderfully foreign and bound for places I have never been.

I HAVE BEEN NOTICING beauty a lot lately. A knock-your-socks-off spring of flowering trees and blooms from every shrub and yard often halt me in my tracks to gaze enraptured at the petal of a dogwood or the way Chartreuse light filters through pale budding leaflets.

How is it that we linger for days and weeks over the latest atrocity and evidence that evil is afoot and keeping steady employment? As a nation, we dissect and examine sin and evil from every angle as we are seduced into complicity by our own fascination with it. We ask the best minds of our day to analyze and respond to iniquity yet rarely consider intently the nature of beauty and how to create and sustain it in our lives and world. Many seek beauty, but it is more often to possess it than to appreciate it. As I impose my will on beauty, as I shape and prune it, cage it in my heart, and bow down and worship it with my reason and money, it becomes a god, something I look to for my well being and satisfaction. Then beauty turns on me with shrewish demands and shrivels into something harsh and burdensome, which sends me off scurrying to polish it, insure it, buy more of it. No more is beauty a source of delight and joy. I have diminished it and myself by my lust, greed, and envy.

A young nurse stammered to tell me of the beauty she had seen last week. "I went for a walk with the dog down by the pond and I have never seen anything like it. After all the rain, the pond was brimming, spilling over the sides. I heard the water roaring through the drainage ditch. I saw God's power, and everything was so green." Tears glistened in her eyes.

True beauty is free. Our spendthrift God scatters it with lavish prodigality over the universe. The Trinity ceaselessly dusts us with beauty like pear blossoms sifting in white drifts on the lawn.

Would that we could approach our lives like kids on an Easter egg hunt at dawn—our world drenched with wonder and surprises nestled under every bush. When Moses was on the far side of the wilderness keeping his father-in-law's flock, he turned aside to see the great sight of the burning bush. What amazes me about Moses is that he turned aside. He stopped doing what he was doing, turned his attention away from his work, and risked letting a sheep wander from his protective gaze, to see why the bush was not burned up (Exod. 3).

Think of it. The liberation of the Hebrews and the rest of salvation history rested on this man's freedom to wonder. The capacity for wonder and curiosity are essential to spiritual growth as well as to justice. A lot of prophets and saints knew how to dilly dally, how to daydream, how to poke along and stop and sniff the odd, the curious and find the hidden treasure under the lilac bush. The expectation and consent to be dazzled and amazed set the stage for God's entrance into our lives.

IN 986 PRINCE VLADIMIR, the pagan ruler of Kiev, decided to make a religious conversion. He was visited by several religious missions representing various faiths. Vladimir was most impressed with the presentation offered by the Greek priest; however, he sent his emissaries to visit a number of neighboring countries to learn how God was worshiped and by whom. They decided that Moslem and Jewish worship beheld no glory and reported to Vladimir, "There is no joy among them, but mournfulness." Traveling next to Germany and Rome, they complained, "There is also a prayer without beauty."

In Constantinople, they attended the Christian worship service in Hagia Sophia, the Cathedral of Holy Wisdom. There they discovered what they sought. One of the prince's emissaries reported: "We know not whether we were in heaven or on earth. For surely on the earth there is no such splendor or such beauty, and we are at a loss to describe it. We know only that God dwells there among people, and their service is fairer than the worship of all other places. We cannot forget the beauty."

How is it that beauty could be the criterion for morality? Beauty, which is in the eye of the beholder and subject to widely varying interpretations and aesthetic understandings, may appear to be an unreliable guide to ultimate reality and right conduct. We are familiar with false beauty, efforts to create a façade that pleases the eye or meets some current standard of popular culture for beauty. Yet, at the same time, we also recognize beauty that fills us with awe, turns us aside, makes us forget sheep who are apt to get themselves into trouble in no time and directs our attention to something compelling, mysterious, and beyond us.

To the willing heart it can happen at any moment:

> Leaning over the newspaper
> I looked up
> and the red shovel
> leaning against the wall
> of the sunporch
> scooped
> a gleaming swath of me,
> and we hung lifted and still.
>
> An illusion,
> this repose on a winter morning,
> for the two of us careening madly
> at fleet velocity collided
> and apprehended
> for a moment
> an eon
> with sweet familiarity
> the web we both comprise.
> Blended we plow the light.

For me, the power of beauty lies in its capacity to redeem. Beauty mends and orders the universe, splintered into trillions of bits and pieces, separate, far flung and broken. Beauty mends and orders me, storm-tossed, sin-sick, and double-minded. Beauty soothes and heals because it reminds me of the interconnectedness of being.

I know and name beauty through my relationship with the world. The Hebrew term for *redeem* carries the notion of one's responsibility to family and right relationship. Redemption is responsible saving action on behalf of another known as an intimate family member. Redemptive beauty affirms that I am not alone but rather am part of something larger than myself to which I am accountable and which sustains me.

To be a soul in wonder is to give oneself to the other—lover, blossom, or eagle—in tender appreciation for the sheer beauty of its existence. I pass out of myself. I set aside my right as an individual in imitation of Christ, who passed out of the Godhead to enter into us, that I might occupy for a moment the pulsing world of the caterpillar or the tumultuous reality of a teenage daughter and thereby touch upon the larger Love that creates and sustains us both.

"The smallest thing touched by love immediately is transfigured and becomes sublime," observed Thomas Merton.[56] Love creates the awareness of beauty, for it is love that gives the grace to appreciate something without needing to possess it. To see the smooth curve of another's impression on reality is in itself a selfless act. This is a looking that does not seek to possess or dominate but merely enters into, appreciates, and walks along side. The universe in all its strangeness and wild variety simply offers its existence to us. As we love it, we find it beautiful. As we find it beautiful, we redeem and are redeemed, for we discover we are not alone but in loving communion with God and all that God has made.

Such spontaneous outflowing of love irresistibly attracted to its manifestation in another is like a dove homing to a place familiar, yet strange, larger than itself, and more beautiful. Or, as Simone Weil wrote, "Beauty is like a mirror that sends us back our own desire for goodness."[57]

"Late have I loved you, Beauty ever ancient, ever new," sighed Augustine, who had long resisted the love of God. Simone Weil declared that beauty is a trap God sets to catch us. She called the beauty of the world "the mouth of the labyrinth" which lures us into the realm of God and Christ's tender smile for us coming through matter.[58]

John of the Cross asked Madre Francisca de la Madre de Dios, "Of what does your prayer consist?" This strikes me as a pretty nosy question of the sort only a spiritual guide might get by with. How do you pray? What is your prayer like? These are intimate questions that many of us would be hard pressed to answer with much precision and clarity. We are more likely to pay attention to the content and timing of our prayers than to the general quality. John's question is really a question about relationship: What is your relationship with God, and how do you experience and express it? Part of the role of a spiritual guide is to help us become aware of the subtlety, nuance, and dynamic of our relationship with the holy.

Mother Francisca answered that her prayer consisted of looking upon God's beauty and rejoicing that God possessed it. Her answer so moved and inspired the little saint that, as the story is reported, he spoke very sublime and wonderful things about the beauty of God for several days. During this time he wrote the final five stanzas of his poem on divine union, *The Spiritual Canticle*, which begin, "Let us rejoice, beloved, and let us go forth to behold ourselves in your beauty."[59]

THE CARDINAL PIERCES the morning with his wet whistle. The columbine bow in the breeze. Diana gets ready for the rock concert. She puts a couple dozen tiny knotted ponytails in her hair so it is sticking out all over. She freshens up her black nail polish. Her T-shirt barely covers her belly button, which she says she wants to pierce. "Well, Mom, how do I look?" she asks.

"Beautiful," I say. So beautiful.

CHAPTER 37

Good-Bye
Change and the Love We Cannot Bear

*Enlarge the site of your tent, and let the curtains of your habitations
be stretched out; do not hold back; lengthen your cords and strengthen
your stakes. For you will spread out to the right and to the left, And your
descendants will possess the nations and will settle the desolate towns.*
— ISAIAH 54:2–3

*W*e were moving, and it wasn't easy on anyone. We had been
coming and going a lot recently. Once in a while Seal slipped
inside the house and wandered from room to room, sniffing
and inspecting. Boxes were everywhere. One day a pile of blankets appeared
on the deck, and the cats draped themselves on old comforters all afternoon. Then out came dolls and stuffed animals, toys, books, and boxes of
old dishes and household items. Early the next morning strangers came,
looked in the boxes, and carried many things away.

Seal knew in her heart that change was coming, and she knew it would
be bad. Ahs barked and strutted. Gavin hid under the deck. Captain
Midnight listened to the pears drop on the deck with a thud, and felt a vague
fear rise in his throat.

"That pear tree is dying," the county extension agent told us seven years
ago. This year the tree held more pears in tight clusters on its limbs than I
have ever seen in our sixteen years here. The trinity of slim maples joined at
the trunk when we came is now over fifteen feet in circumference. Its
branches canopy the backyard with green leaf lace. I see in flickering shadows
memories of tricycles, swings, a tree house, sandbox, and diapers flapping in
the breeze. I wonder in my tears if the sorrow of good-byes is not so much loss

of something loved as the awareness gained of what has been intolerably beautiful and good in our lives.

Love, like millions of particles of dancing light, penetrates every second of our existence, but most of it passes through us as indiscernible as air. We do not see what we would die without. In our good-byes the contours of grace rise in stark relief against the backdrop of our lives. Then we see what was hidden or only dimly known: how very great is the goodness we've been given, and how tenderly we have been cared for by our God.

Nothing shows us love so clearly as death, or threat of loss. I saw an ad for K-Mart on TV this fall. A little kid on his way to kindergarten sagely observes, "Everyone has to leave home; that is how you learn about the Force." And William Blake wrote, "We are put on earth a little space to learn to bear the beams of love."[60] Love requires bearing in the sense of tolerating its depth and breadth, holding up under the weight of goodness. When St. Catherine asked if she could see God, the Creator declined, telling her that if she saw God's glory, she would die from such a blessing. Maybe part of the pain we feel in leave-taking is the tearing of our hearts as they are enlarged to encompass previously unknown graces. Our dwelling place in creation, the place our hearts call home, where we find our comfort and safety, is stretched wider and wider by each good-bye to encompass more and more of God's truth and love.

It is in the being of the days that a thing makes sense, the clear, confusing, giddy, dull, and tearful passing of the time.

On one of the last evenings at our home in Holton, I took a walk. I went down the block past the schools, around the city lake, up the hill beside the park, through the neighborhood. I was flooded with memories of friends, events, and families—and a strange affection for the brick streets. No different from millions of pathways throughout the world, why were these streets and walks so dear? Perhaps because they bore what my heart could not without breaking: the weight of lives lived with all the courage and dignity they could muster.

I counted seven persons who had died in my neighborhood while we lived there. Who could tell the suffering, quiet heroism, and joy these streets bore? I remembered with a smile my excruciatingly bumpy ride over those bricks to the hospital where Cicelia was born ten minutes after we arrived.

When I returned home from my walk, I picked up a wide strip of masking tape in the front yard next to the "For Sale" sign. "Home is here only!" it read in defiant blue letters. I think I know who wrote these words. I think

I know whose fiercely loving heart is facing its first deep loss and at an age when she lacks the jaundiced perspective of years of good-byes. For her, home is not where the heart is but here only, because here is the only place her heart has ever been. She is learning about the force of a love which continually coaxes us to enlarge our sites.

Like God in Jesus Christ, we are made vulnerable and holy by what we love and lay our hearts out for. We wind our passion like a satin bow round what we see as beloved and worthy in our lives. Then, in a thousand different ways, God calls us to let go and move on—hurricane, earthquake, bullet, stroke, aircraft which falls out of the sky. You might avoid some of the pain by remaining aloof, detached, and cynical. You can keep your heart locked in a box, stay away from churches, mystery, and wonder, but sooner or later God makes broken-hearted lovers out of all us.

Perhaps it takes a lifetime for us to get over the scandal of our vulnerability—to stop apologizing for it or trying to deny or hide it, to stop trotting off to plastic surgeons and swilling down elixirs of eternal youth, to stop trying to pin our hopes and happiness on anything less than God. Or maybe we are given the time of our lives for this very purpose: to be stretched by love, best known and felt in its letting go; to have our hearts spread wide as Christ's arms spread upon the cross; to lengthen our heartstrings and drive our tent stakes past the things of this world, down deep into the solid rock of God.

AFTER WEEKS OF WORRYING, the animals found themselves in the back of a speeding car, racing through the dark to an unknown land. Seal's voice rose in a long, anguished caterwaul. Gavin peered worriedly through the mesh of the cage but remained silent, while Seal paced and chewed at the wire, poking her paws through the holes.

Finally, the car came to a stop, and the sound of the motor died. A door opened, and the cage was lifted up and carried into the light. They were inside a strange house with many new smells. Gavin cowered in a corner. Seal renewed her protest with fresh urgency. "Where are we? Why are we here? I want to go home!"

Can you take home with you when you move? Can you put holiness in a box and haul it after you? In ancient times our mothers and fathers hauled the Ark of the Covenant back and forth across the desert. Today a woman gestures toward the row of photos on her dresser. "There is my family. Eight grandchildren," she proudly tells me. "This painting my husband did just before he died. And this oak table belonged to my grandfather." Amid possessions reduced to a few dresses in the small closet and what this room can hold, she sits serene as a nun. "I am ready to go, to die any time now," she says with a quiet smile.

We are only as happy as the depth of our trust in God. The spiritual journey is a long and painful weaning of our trust in and love for anything that is not God.

WHEN JOHN KENNEDY, JR. died in a plane crash, I wept, "I do not want it to be so," over and over. The brevity of our days, the apparent ultimate inconsequence of things I value most in the immense sweep of time, the paradoxical worth of a human being whom God loves and moves through to bless and redeem, one small life in the vast sea of human existence, billions of people, billions of years. *May it not be so*—this vulnerability, this life subject to futility. *May it not be so*—that human power and control are fleeting at best, and an illusion a good deal of the time. *May it not be so.*

Yet we all go down to the grave. Good-byes in greater and lesser degree confront us with the alarming truth of which most of the time we have not a clue: that we are totally dependent on God and that any ground other than God on which we may attempt to find a foothold is nothing more than shifting sand. Staking one's heart and life on eternity is the only safe sure bet. And how precarious that is, resting solely on faith.

God shows us in our grief and fear what it might be time for us to let go of. Anxiety and sorrow may reveal where we are unconsciously placing our trust, instead of in God. In this case grief is partly the loss of an illusion, the sadness over the failure of something or someone not being what it never could have been or was meant to be in the first place.

> First my creatures find me in love—in love with one another, in love of creation, its treasures and wonders. Then my creatures are able to separate me from what I have made. They find me, who, clothed with the robe of creation, beckons and woos them through the delights of this world. Slowly I unveil myself, as I strip from them anything that is not true and eternal. They begin to recognize what is unseen as what is Real, and they learn my name is Faith. The less they hold onto in this world, the more of eternity I can pour through them into the present and the greater our joy will be.

PEARS LITTER THE GROUND beneath the tree at our old home. I've come back to get the last few things. The air is sweet with the heady scent of sun-warmed pears ripening to dark soft skins. I don't see them at first in the slants of sun across the brown leaves and yellow fruit. After I have been sitting on the ground breathing in pear musk for a while, something moves. A brown leaf opens, closes. Opens again. A mottled orange flame leaps up and then goes out. Orange flame. Brown leaf. Orange flame. Another and another, dozens of flickering votives beneath the pear tree. Tiny feet clinging to pears, wings opening and closing like breath. Inhale—wings close; exhale—wings open. Feeding, supping up the sweet juice. I remember another time years before when the monarchs came and rested all night in the leaves of the pear tree. How many times had they come to feed since and I had not seen them?

Life is all too wonderful for us to bear. So put your whole body down on this good earth and feed on the sweetness of the One who hung from a tree and in whose dying we find life in our dying.

Faith rises in a thin blue stream of smoke from the ashes of our lives, weaving its way through the chill autumn night toward heaven. Enlarge your tent, drive your stakes into the substance of things hoped for, the assurance of things unseen.

> On Christ the solid rock we stand.
> All other ground is shifting sand.
> All other ground is shifting sand.[61]

THAT FIRST NIGHT Seal and Gavin hid in the woods. In the morning we found them cringing on the roof while Ahs paced below. Then Gavin disappeared for a whole week. But now the cats and Captain Midnight have settled in on the deck at their new home, and Ahs is busy herding anything that moves. The sumac is blood-red on the hillsides. In the woods I find hickory nuts, walnuts, and bittersweet. Deer come into the clearing at dusk. A screech owl sings his fluttering song in the darkness.

Captain has started to pull in his legs and grow still and recollected as Isabella used to do. Things hadn't been right since Isabella died in the damp chill of early spring. Mourning Dove said it was like that with those who loved God too much. "They burn up and go to an early grave like some of the saints," she said.

If that was true, Captain wished Isabella had loved God less. He missed her beautiful, kind eyes, her companionship, and her wisdom. What would she say about all this? he wondered. "Have faith," he thought; she'd say,

"Have faith." He wasn't sure what faith was and he was pretty sure he didn't have any, unless it was somewhere under the straw in the back of his pen.

He thinks all that over as he washes his ears. Then he wiggles his nose and takes a big bite out of the carrot he found hidden under the straw this morning. He isn't sure what faith is, but carrots are the assurance of things hoped for, the conviction of things unseen.

CHAPTER 38

Faith and Fear
Ahs Gets a New Home

*A*hs, I have faith that you can do this. It is not that hard. Look, it is warm and cozy inside. There is plenty of room. Your old blanket is in here, and some nice soft hay. Come on, Ahs.

The dog paces nervously, stops, and tilts his head to one side. Then he goes over to the rug on the porch and lies down.

"No, Ahs. Come here. This is your new house!" I am down on all fours before the doghouse. "Watch me, Ahs. Do it like this." I crawl inside the house, turn around, curl up, and poke my head out. The dog watches me curiously. He thumps his tail encouragingly on the porch as if to say, "Good human!"

The doghouse came with our new home. Painted to match and built to last, the house is warm and dry. I am determined to coax Ahs to move in, but he is afraid. This is why I am scraping my spine on the opening, wedging my knees to my chin, and squeezing into a doghouse. This is why I stashed a dog treat in the back of his house, why I even crammed in the doghouse with a turkey gizzard and a stinky sock. I want to help Ahs overcome his fear and find comfortable lodging for the winter. But he prefers to tough out the cold nights huddled on a rug on the porch.

At some point, crammed in the doghouse with a turkey gizzard in one hand and a stinky sock in the other, thoughts of God enter my mind. The parallel of the Almighty stooping to enter earth's cramped quarters in order to show us the way to abundant life does not escape me.

Fear holds a good many of us, like Ahs, on the threshold of the house of the Lord, pacing back and forth, wringing our hands, wondering if we can just go in and make ourselves at home and know everything will be all right. What if the invitation to well-being and abundance is a trap? The rug on the porch is familiar. Tolerating misery may be more comfortable than tolerating uncertainty and surrendering to new circumstances.

MOST EVERY EPIPHANY or showing of God in Scriptures is met with fear. When the angel Gabriel comes to Mary saying, "Rejoice, O highly favored one; the Lord is with you," Mary does not break out in ecstatic bliss. Instead she is greatly troubled at the saying. As Luke tells it, she considers in her mind what sort of greeting this might be. And well she might. It was probably not the first time some itinerant ladies' man claiming to be an angel had come on to her.

The angels in the Bible get some of the worst lines. They are hard to pull off with any authenticity. Enter one angel Gabriel with a flourish of wings and heavenly splendor who must make believable both his incredible presence and the words: "Rejoice, O favored one." Smile, God loves you. This is your lucky day! Any virgin with an ounce of sense might consider in her mind, "Right, Sweetie. Have I ever heard that one before."

The immensity of the heavens is about to invade her in a mysterious and awesome conception that will defy rational explanation and accomplish an incarnation that ushers in the redemption of the world. Yet before Christ is born, Mary must face her fear and make a choice. And so it is with us. When God's cheery messenger meets us with the news that we will conceive and bring forth the fruit of salvation, fear rather than joy is likely to be our first response.

Messengers sent by God to announce God's saving love often wear camouflage. They have a hundred disguises. Can we trust that they are who they say they are? This seed of hope they want to place within us, dare we believe it, receive it? What if we are mistaken and this is all a dream or a product of our own egotistical imaginations? What arrogance makes you think you can bear salvific fruit, sacred saving gifts to the world? This is no angel, but Cousin Carl dressed up in Aunt Edith's chenille bathrobe with some tinfoil wings and a halo made out of a pie pan.

In real life angels rarely look like the ones in paintings. And yet, does it matter if the angel really is Cousin Carl? To me, what matters is that we believe that holiness and salvation are afoot, whatever ridiculous disguises they wear. Prior to the advent of God's redeeming love in our lives and in our world comes a courageous act of faith. The birth of Christ is contingent on the belief of a young girl with an imagination creative enough to envision the impossible and a sense of her worth strong enough to defy fear and anxiety. She places her whole being in jeopardy as she lays out her life and all that she holds dear on the gamble that there is a God in the heaven who might have some business to do with her.

We are to rely on faith rather than evidence, Iain Matthew writes in his interpretation of St. John of the Cross. Yet, here's the kicker: the danger St. John warns of "is not so much that we shall trust in the wrong thing, but that we shall stop trusting at all; that, while we may never say it in so many words, we shall cease to believe that we are a factor in God's life."[62]

Matthew continues:

> Survival demands a certain skepticism. We are trained to cope as social beings by keeping our desires within realistic limits. But where God is concerned, the problem lies in our desiring too little, and growing means expanding our expectations; or rather, making [God's] generosity, not our poverty, the measure of our expectations.[63]

Mary, sizing up her heavenly visitor, is moving from the rather safe place of conventional norms into a new realm where few of the old rules will make much sense. No one else can judge for her the validity of that grinning angel holding out joy like Aunt Lucille's fruitcake. Should she take a bite? She hasn't forgotten that incident in the garden with the serpent. What is truth? How can she be sure this is an invitation from God?

There are no books she can read, no wise men and women she can consult. She alone must determine and act on her own truth. How will Joseph or her village ever believe what is happening to her? Yet what others will think is not her ultimate concern. Her concern is obedience to the living God, to hope, to the possibility of wonder that lies beyond what the eye can see. Joseph and the others must come to their own conclusions. They, along with the rest of us, are given that freedom. In W. H. Auden's poem "For the Time Being" Joseph says to Gabriel:

> All I ask is one
> important and elegant proof
> That what my Love had done
> Was really at your will
> And that your will is Love.
> Gabriel responds:
> No, you must believe;
> Be silent and sit still.[64]

Weighing the odds, Mary asks one question, "How shall this be since I have no husband?" "No problem," guarantees the angel. And citing the case of barren Elizabeth, he assures her that with God nothing is impossible. Mary's question raises a far from minor point. The participation of a male is a basic ingredient for conception. When God sends a divine messenger to us announcing that we have been chosen to bring forth some saving work, it may appear that some major components for success have been omitted. How shall this be since I have no money? Since I have no work? Since I have no education?

"No worry, it'll be a cinch," says Cousin Carl, snapping his fingers. "The Holy Spirit will come upon you."

Finally it is up to Mary. The redemption of the cosmos is resting on the consent, the free choice of this mortal woman to have faith, to believe that what she is experiencing is true, and to claim and live out her experience of that truth by conceiving the fruit of salvation.

Mary takes hold of, seizes, the inconceivable. The purity and faith of the virgin penetrate the illusion and falsity that surround her, and she offers her whole being—intellect, imagination, heart, and body—to deliver redemption into her world. She claims her power as the mother of redemption and joins with God in a dance of saving love. That same dance has the power to transform Cousin Carl with acne and Aunt Edith with her hair in curlers into the heavenly hosts and you and me into bearers of Christ.

Do you see the mutuality in this exchange of love between a mortal and the Holy One? The prophet Zephaniah calls Israel to rejoice because God is in her midst; he further proclaims that this God in her midst is rejoicing over her with gladness (3:14–18). Israel rejoices over God. God rejoices over Israel. God chooses Mary. Mary chooses God. We long for peace and wholeness. God longs to give us peace and wholeness.

What prevents more of this dancing in our lives and world? A significant impediment must be our fear.

IN THE STORY of Christ's birth, several of the players are exhorted not to fear—Zechariah, Mary, Joseph, the shepherds. The gospel writers over twenty times show Jesus admonishing others not to fear. Fear may be seen as one of the indicators of the presence of God. Fear of God, which is the human response to God's overpowering majesty, glory, and power, is an appropriate and desired reaction. In contrast, fear of the world, fear of self and others, is seen as counterproductive to God's action in our lives.

Beatrice Bruteau writes of faith as an attitude of the consciousness that is participating in divine activity, God's creative work in the world. Faith is "the disposition which Jesus declared to be a condition for the realization of his works. The doer of the work had to have faith, and the receiver of the work had to have faith." She considers faith as "not only the consent of the intellect to the reality of something that does not appear immediately to the sense, but it is the consent of the imagination and the affective faculties attached to the imagination."[65] Thus, the new thing God is doing enters this world—

as we agree something better is possible,
as we are able to vividly envision the new thing,
as we feel in our hearts the joy and delight of that yet unborn promise,
as we persevere in that vision in the face of fear and threats,
and as we live expectantly as if the vision is accomplished.

FEAR KEEPS US STUCK in the present reality, constricted and paralyzed by the very thing God is setting about to redeem. Fear distracts us from watching and waiting eagerly for the in-breaking of God's promises into the world. Fear turns our eyes away from the coming Bridegroom to become mesmerized by the horror of a realm that does not know God. Fear, then, may be seen as faith in your enemy.

The danger, as Matthews writes, "is of folding in on oneself. Pain does that, and the temptation is to look for a both/and: both staying with the new setting, and feeding on nostalgia for the old one. Unhappily this both/and tends to backfire. We cannot both indulge self-pity and make the most of a new situation."[66] In other words, you cannot both sleep on the porch and snuggle in the doghouse next to a turkey gizzard.

Simply put, our faith allows Christ to enter the world. Think for a moment. How do you feel when someone expresses faith in you? When another trusts you and has faith in your gifts, are you not enlarged, empowered, more willing to offer your gifts? Perhaps the reason why Jesus urges his followers to have faith, why he shakes his head in dismay at the disciples' doubts and fear, is that their faith in Jesus empowered Jesus.

So, as Annie Dillard writes: "Faith, crucially, is not assenting intellectually to a series of doctrinal propositions; it is living in conscious and rededicated relationship with God."[67] Further, faith is not a vague and wispy sense that God is out there somewhere looking on us with a benevolent eye, nor is it an exercise of philosophical proofs. Faith is the means by which God enters and changes our reality. Faith is an interactive experience, a dance of mutual love between a mortal and God in which both parties are needed, affected, and changed for the benefit of the whole world.

AHS IS STILL SLEEPING on the porch along side his doghouse. His master tells me it is because he is holding out for moving inside with us. He says the dog has faith and is persisting in his vision of a nice cozy spot on the couch and standing firm in the face of all distractions no matter how tasty and stinky they may be.

EPILOGUE

• • •

$\mathcal{B}$utterscotch died in late spring of 1997, a few days before we made the long drive from Kansas to the high desert of New Mexico. A neighbor's dog jumped against her cage pushing in one side and frightening her. The golden rex rabbit broke her spine, went into shock, and died a few hours later.

That fall the rabbits, Isabella and Captain Midnight, joined the household. Beautiful Isabella, with her recollected soul, lived only two years before she succumbed to a virus and died.

Grace, by its very nature, cannot survive violence. Neither can we, who are sanctuaries of grace. Nor, in spite of our best efforts, can we always preserve purity, innocence, and goodness. Though violence destroys grace, grace is ever replenished by God's mercy.

After Butterscotch died, I took her body, wrapped in a towel by my grieving daughter, and sat on the porch swing. We rocked where we had rocked so many times before. In grief as sharp as any I had known, I sang her the lullabies I sang my daughters when they were babies. Then, glancing out across the lawn, I caught the shadowy form of a rabbit ascending in a series of glad leaps, bounding up the sweet night air.

Slow down. Find your way to Turtle Street. We have eternity, you know.

ENDNOTES

• • •

1. Gerald May, *Will and Spirit* (San Francisco: Harper & Row, 1987), ch. 5.
2. Evelyn Underhill, *Mysticism* (New York: Meridian Books, 1957), 381.
3. Prov. 8:29–31, author's paraphrase.
4. "Unless devotion is given to the thing which must prove false in the end, that which is true in the end cannot enter." Charles Williams, *He Came Down from Heaven* (London: Faber and Faber, 1950), 25.
5. John of the Cross, *The Ascent of Mount Carmel*, Bk. II, Ch. 22, 5, in *The Collected Works of St. John of the Cross*, trans. Kieran Kavanaugh and Otilio Rodriguez (Washington, D.C.: ICS Publications, 1973), 180.
6. Simone Weil, *Waiting for God* (New York: Harper Colophon Books), 69.
7. The Larger Catechism 7.111, as found in *The Constitution of the Presbyterian Church (USA), Book of Confessions.*
8. John of the Cross, *The Spiritual Canticle*, in *Collected Works*, 434.
9. Weil, *Waiting for God*, 190.
10. As told in Zalman M. Schachter and Edward Hoffman, *Sparks of Light: Counseling in the Hasidic Tradition* (Boulder and London: Shambhala, 1983), 119.
11. Evelyn Underhill, *Concerning the Inner Life* (Minneapolis: The Seabury Press, 1926), 140–141.
12 Baron von Hügel, *Spiritual Counsel and Letters of Friedrich von Hügel*, ed. Douglas V. Steere (New York and Evanston, Harper & Row) as quoted in *Spiritual Disciplines for Everyday Living*, ed. Ronald V. Wells (Bridgeport, CT: DC Books,1987), 102–103.
13. Underhill, *Concerning the Inner Life*, 140.
14. A reference to Isaiah 55:1: "Ho, everyone who thirsts come to the waters; and you that have no money, come, buy and eat!"

15. John Calvin, *Institutes of the Christian Religion*, ed. John T. McNeill, trans. Ford Lewis Battles (Philadelphia: Westminster Press, 1960), I.1.10, 253; I.1.2, 38; I.1.8, 251.
16. John of the Cross, *The Living Flame of Love*, in *Collected Works*, 645.
17. Thomas Merton, *The Sign of Jonas* (New York: Harcourt, Brace and Company, 1953), 268.
18. Walter Brueggemann, *Genesis* (Atlanta: John Knox Press, 1982), 56.
19. Ibid.
20. Walter Wink, "Prayer," *Sojourners* (October 1990), 10.
21. I first heard this quotation in a video on professional boundary violations by clergy. It was attributed to a Jewish writer, whose name I do not know. I am indebted to David R. Blumenthal, *Facing the Abusing God—A Theology of Protest* (Louisville: Westminster/John Knox, 1993), for some of the ideas in this chapter.
22. Underhill, *Mysticism*, 14.
23. Kathleen Fischer, "Spiritual Direction with Women," *The Handbook of Spirituality for Ministers*, ed. Robert J. Wicks (New York: Paulist Press, 1995), 104.
24. I am indebted to Johanna Bos and Phyllis Trible for some of the ideas in this chapter.
25. Fischer, "Spiritual Direction with Women," 104.
26. As found in *The Merriam-Webster Dictionary of Quotations* (Springfield, MA: Merriam-Webster, Inc., 1992), 53.
27. Quoted by Paul Mariani in an address given on August 19, 1995, in Colorado Springs.
28. See note 7.
29. M. Basil Pennington, *Call to the Center* (Hyde Park, NY: New City Press, 1995), 35.
30. "When I shall cleave to Thee with all my being, then shall I in nothing have pain and labour; and my life shall be a real life, being wholly full of Thee." St. Augustine, *Confessions*, Book 10, as quoted in Underhill, *Mysticism*, 420.
31. Lesslie Newbigin, *Truth to Tell, The Gospel as Public Truth* (Grand Rapids, MI: Eerdmans, 1991), 29–30.
32. Ibid., 51.
33. Evelyn Underhill in letter to Cosmo Gordon Land, the Archbishop of Canterbury, about the inner life of clergy, as published in *The Christian Century* (October 31, 1990): 998.
34. Quoted in *Ministry of Money*, #102 (June 1969).

35. Address given by John Dominic Crossan at the Trinity Institute, 1995.
36. As quoted in Robert F. Morneau, *From Resurrection to Pentecost* (New York: The Crossroad Publishing Company, 2000), 68.
37. Evagrius Ponticus, as quoted in Louis Bouyer, *A History of Christian Spirituality, The Spirituality of the New Testament and the Fathers* (New York: Desclee Co., 1963), 385.
38. Underhill, *Mysticism*, 394.
39. Meister Eckhart, *Meditations with Meister Eckhart*, versions by Matthew Fox (Santa Fe: Bear & Company, 1983), 50.
40. John of the Cross, *The Dark Night*, in *Collected Works*, 302.
41. Henri Nouwen, "Time Enough to Minister," in *Leadership* (Spring 1982).
42. Evelyn Underhill, *The House of the Soul* (Minneapolis: The Seabury Press, 1929), 112.
43 John of the Cross, *The Dark Night*, in *Collected Works*, 371.
44 Dag Hammarskjöld, *Markings*, trans. Leif Sjoberg and W. H. Auden (New York: Alfred A. Knopf, 1966), 174.
45. Thomas H. Green, S.J., *When the Well Runs Dry*, new rev. ed. (Notre Dame, IN: Ave Maria Press, 1998), 160.
46. John of the Cross, *Ascent to Mt. Carmel*, in *Collected Works*, 68.
47. Thomas Merton, *Reflections of a Guilty Bystander* (Garden City, NY: Image Books, 1968), 86.
48. Matthew 6:6, in Eugene Peterson, *The Message: The New Testament in Contemporary English* (Colorado Springs: Navpress, 1993).
49. See note 30 above.
50. *The Merriam-Webster Dictionary of Quotations*, 246.
51. Brenda Ueland, *If You Want to Write* (St. Paul: Graywolf Press, 1987), 32.
52. Fyodor Dostoevsky, *The Brothers Karamazov*, trans. Constance Garnett (New York: Random House, Inc., 1966), 60.
53. Walter Brueggemann, *The Land* (Philadelphia: Fortress Press, 1977), 67–69.
54. Weil, *Waiting for God*, 195–196.
55. From the hymn "Amazing Grace," by John Newton.
56. Merton, *Sign of Jonas*, 186.
57. Weil, *Waiting for God*, 166.
58. Weil, *Waiting for God*, 163–164.
59. St. John of the Cross, *The Spiritual Canticle*, in *Collected Works*, 414.
60. William Blake, "The Little Black Boy."
61. From the hymn "My Hope Is Built," by Edward Mote.

62. Iain Matthew, *The Impact of God–Soundings from St. John of the Cross*, (London: Hodder and Stoughton Ltd., 1995), 32.
63. Ibid., 32–33.
64. W. H. Auden, "For the Time Being, A Christmas Oratorio".
65. *Beatrice Bruteau,* "Prayer: Insight and Manifestation," *Contemplative Review* (Fall 1983), 38.
66. Matthews, *The Impact of God*, 89.
67. Annie Dillard, *For the Time Being* (New York: Alfred A. Knopf, 1999), 146.